JB
KENNEDY

12/01

$26.90

Landau, Elaine.

John F. Kennedy, Jr.

DATE			

John F. Kennedy Jr.

John F. Kennedy Jr.

by Elaine Landau

Twenty-First Century Books   Brookfield, Connecticut

For Derek Kessler

Title page photographs in montage courtesy of (clockwise from top left): John F. Kennedy Library, Stanley Tretick/Corbis-Sygma, James Andanson & Alain Nogues/Sygma, Grace/Sygma, © Bettmann/Corbis, Tanenbaum/Sygma, Kevin Galin/Sygma

Photographs courtesy of AP/Wide World Photos: pp. 6, 55 (bottom), 94, 97, 98, 106 (top), Skytech, Inc.: p. 11 (top); © Liaison Agency: pp. 11 (bottom), 67, 88 (top, Ansin), 91 (Stephen Ferry); © Corbis-Sygma: pp. 21 (Ira Wyman), 31 (Stanley Tretick), 40 (Stanley Tretick), 76 (top left, Zarcoff), 83 (bottom, Ira Wyman), 93 (top, Rick Maiman), 101 (Mark Alesky), 113 (right, Brooks Kraft); Bill Greene/*The Boston Globe*: p. 22; © Bettmann/Corbis: pp. 24, 29, 76 (bottom); Corbis/Bettmann-UPI: pp. 47, 59, 76 (top right), 83 (top), 93 (bottom), 112-113; Everett Collection: p. 55 (top); *Women's Wear Daily*: p. 62; M. Riordan/ Photofest: p. 70 'PEOPLE' Weekly is a registered trademark of Time Inc., used with permission: p. 88 (bottom); © Denis Reggie: p. 105; © David Allen/Corbis: p. 106 (bottom); John F. Kennedy Library/SIPA: pp. 108-109

Library of Congress Cataloging-in-Publication Data
Landau, Elaine.
John F. Kennedy Jr. / by Elaine Landau.
    p. cm.
Includes bibliographical references and index.
Summary: A biography of the son of the thirty-fifth president of the United States, discussing his toddler days in the White House, "America's Most Eligible Bachelor," the launching of his political magazine "George," and his death in an airplane crash at the age of thirty-eight.
ISBN 0-7613-1857-7 (lib. bdg.)
1. Kennedy, John F. (John Fitzgerald), 1960– —Juvenile literature.
2. Children of presidents—United States—Biography—Juvenile literature. [1. Kennedy, John F. (John Fitzgerald), 1960- 2. Children of presidents.] I. Title.
E843.L36 2000   973.922'092—dc21   [B]00-027659

Published by Twenty-First Century Books
A Division of The Millbrook Press, Inc.
2 Old New Milford Road
Brookfield, Connecticut 06804
www.millbrookpress.com

Contents

John F. Kennedy Jr. and Carolyn Bessette.
*All of America fell in love with this magical couple
when they fell in love with each other.*

Chapter 1

It Should Have Been...

F riday . . .

July 16, 1999 . . .

It should have been a wonderful weekend. One of America's most glamorous couples was to fly their private plane to Cape Cod for a family wedding. Everything this couple did was news. They were the essence of youth, beauty, and adventure in a country that prized these qualities. They were continually plagued by paparazzi, and photos of the pair sold for thousands of dollars. They were the couple that young Americans wanted to be or be with. They were John F. Kennedy Jr. and his wife, Carolyn Bessette Kennedy.

JFK Jr. was a young man who seemed to have it all. The son of the 35th president of the United States, he proved to be a dashing figure in his own right. Possessing good looks, considerable wealth, and a famous family name, it appeared as if the world was at his feet. Few doors were closed to him, and many Americans hoped that he would follow in his father's footsteps and one day become president. However, it's doubtful that John was thinking about the presidency that Friday. Friends say he was looking forward to the wedding and his trip to Cape Cod. One noted in describing John's mood at the start of the weekend: "He was in a fine state of mind. He was at the height of himself."[1]

There was another reason for John's lighthearted mood that day. Only the day before, he had a cast removed from his left ankle. He had broken his ankle during a paragliding accident on Memorial Day weekend, and the injury had kept the sports-loving Kennedy from skating, biking, kayaking, and, perhaps most important, flying the new plane he had bought only months before.

Flying was a cherished passion. He put off pilot lessons until after his mother's death, as she firmly believed that flying was too risky a hobby. Yet Kennedy later took to the air like a bird freed from its cage. "He said it was the most fun he ever had with his clothes on," recalled Richard Wiese, a college buddy. "It was just him up there, away from everybody, and it made him feel free."[2] These feelings were echoed by Arthur Marx, one of Kennedy's flight instructors, who noted early on that the young man would "rather be flying than working." When Marx saw Kennedy carefully washing his new plane, he commented: "You know how it is when you get a new car? He was picking little pieces of dust off it."[3]

The plane was a red-and-white single-engine, six-seat Piper 32 Saratoga—a high performance plane with a good safety record. JFK Jr. purchased it second-hand for about $300,000. There were some, however, who felt that Kennedy did not have sufficient flight experience to pilot the aircraft. The plane's power coupled with its complex autopilot system might have been beyond his grasp at that point in his flight training. "Our company would have never sold that airplane to that man," John Foster, president of SkyTech Inc., an authorized distributor of Piper Aircraft, later commented. "We wouldn't have sold it to him for a million dollars."[4]

By 1998, Kennedy had earned his private pilot's license. However, he still lacked an instrument rating, which meant that he was not qualified to fly in conditions that necessitated instrument navigation.

Nevertheless, it looked initially as though conditions on the evening of July 16 might be suitable for a pilot of his rating, and Kennedy was anxious to take to the air again. In less than twenty-four hours he thought he would be at his family's compound in Hyannis Port, Massachusetts, joking with his thirty-year-old cousin Rory Kennedy about becoming a married woman.

*J*ohn's thirty-three-year-old wife, Carolyn Bessette Kennedy, was busy preparing for the trip that Friday. The tall blonde had some last-minute shopping to do before going away for the weekend. She still didn't have a dress for the ceremony on Saturday, and there wasn't much time left to find one. That afternoon she headed for the fashionable department store Saks Fifth Avenue where she spotted what she was looking for. It was a glamorous black silk crepe evening dress with a designer label.

Just after 6:30 P.M., she hopped into a car service limo and headed for the Essex County Airport in nearby New Jersey, where she would meet her husband and sister. Carolyn's sister, Lauren Bessette, would be flying with them; the couple planned to drop her off at Martha's Vineyard (an island just off the southeast coast of Massachusetts) before going on to Hyannis Port for the wedding. The Bessette sisters had grown especially close in recent months after Lauren purchased an apartment in a luxury high-rise building just two blocks from the young Kennedy couple. Besides being John's sister-in-law, Lauren Bessette had another connection to the Kennedy family: She had recently begun dating television producer Robert Shriver, another of John's cousins.

That evening John picked up Lauren after work to drive to the airport. Lauren was employed at the investment firm of Dean Witter & Co., only blocks from where John worked, so it was easy for her brother-in-law to stop by for her in his car. By about 6:45 P.M. the pair was on the road, but congested weekend traffic lengthened the trip and they didn't reach the airport until nearly 8:00 P.M.

John's cast was off, but he was still on crutches. On his way to the airport he stopped at a gas station. The attendant there saw Kennedy's crutches and wondered about the celebrity's ability to maneuver the car's pedals. "How he drove, I don't know," he would later wonder.[5] Yet in less than an hour, John would pilot a plane. This time he would be the solo pilot, though in the past Kennedy often flew to Martha's Vineyard with a flight instructor on board. Earlier that week he had flown to Canada with a flight instructor, and the previous weekend he and Carolyn had a flight instructor with them when they brought another couple up to Martha's Vineyard as their guests. But without his cast and a little more pilot experience behind him, Kennedy now felt he could handle things on his own.

Not everyone, however, had a great deal of faith in this still somewhat inexperienced pilot. In a May 1998 interview, Kennedy admitted that few of his relatives would fly with him. "The only person I've been able to get to go up with me, who looks forward to it as much as I do, is my wife," he said. "The second it was legal she came up with me. [Now] whenever we want to get away, we can just get in a plane and fly off."[6]

John's Piper Saratoga, such as the one shown above, was
a powerful, high-performance aircraft equipped with all the amenities.
But on the night of July 16, as the haze deepened and darkness fell,
the plane might just as well have been windowless.

Lauren Bessette, who
was riding with Carolyn in the
leather seats behind the cockpit,
had been virtually unknown to
the public—until the tragic
summer weekend that would
forever link her name with those
of her famous sister and
brother-in-law.

But Carolyn Kennedy's enthusiasm may have waned over time, since John was later quoted as saying, "Nobody likes flying with me, including my wife…. I'm no Charles Lindbergh."[7] It had also been noted by some close to the couple that Carolyn frequently drove from New York to Martha's Vineyard on weekends to avoid flying with her husband. On some occasions, she even flew up in a separate chartered plane.

Nevertheless, that evening both his wife and his sister would be passengers on the Piper Saratoga, even though flying conditions had begun to deteriorate. By the time the plane had been checked, fueled, and readied for takeoff, it was after 8:30 P.M. That meant flying at night, and to worsen matters a thick haze had settled over the area. Given the darkness and haze and the fact that John was still on crutches and did not yet have his pilot's instrument rating, there might have been cause for concern.

Warren Moringstar, a pilot and spokesman for the Aircraft Owners and Pilots Association, described the situation this way: "What the pilot wants to have is a relatively distinct horizon, to see the ground and be able to determine the aircraft's altitude by looking outside. At night your visual horizon is not going to be as distinct, and if it's hazy your vision is going to be obscured."[8] Martha's Vineyard was known for its thick summer haze and fog, and that evening was no exception.

No one will ever know precisely what occurred in the plane that night. We do know that Kennedy took off at 8:38 P.M. from Runway 22—twelve minutes after sunset. His recent ankle injury was probably not a problem since the takeoff went smoothly. Kennedy then headed east across the Hudson River toward Long Island Sound. As expected, his plane climbed to an altitude of 5,600 feet (1,707 m). To his left, Kennedy would have seen lights from the towns along Connecticut's southern coast.

It's likely that the traveling trio were comfortable inside the plane. The positions of the bodies at the crash site suggest that Carolyn and her sister were at the rear of the cabin while John was at the controls. The young women may have been talking. The overhead lights in that part of the plane would have allowed them to do some reading as well.

Yet by 9:26 P.M. the mood on board might have changed. John must have realized that the haze surrounding the plane had thickened. Under good weather conditions, to his right, Kennedy ordinarily would have seen the outline of Block Island. On the left, he would have seen lights from the town of Westerly, Rhode Island. But none of this was visible through the haze.

Radar indicates that while Kennedy's plane had remained at a steady altitude of 5,600 feet, at this point it began to descend at a rate of 700 feet (213 m) per minute—a faster-than-usual speed for a single-engine aircraft. There is speculation that Kennedy could have been trying to fly below the haze. In any case, the small plane's fairly rapid descent continued for about five minutes until Kennedy was flying at an altitude of only 2,300 feet (700 m) above the water. Ideally, he should have been able to look out the window to get his bearings, but the haze made that impossible.

Dr. Bob Arnot, an NBC medical correspondent, who had flown his private plane to Cape Cod less than an hour before Kennedy took off, described what conditions were like that night: "When I looked down on Martha's Vineyard, I could not see it. I saw nothing. It's as if somebody put you in a closet and shut the door. I haven't seen conditions like that for years. I have 5,000 hours [of flying time] and I had a problem."[9]

By then Kennedy had probably performed what pilots call "the scan," a quick review of the instrument board, which ideally would have enabled him to determine the craft's altitude and direction. But as Kennedy still lacked his pilot's instrument rating, these tools may not have been of much help in what was rapidly becoming a confusing and perhaps unnerving situation.

Kennedy was only about 10 to 20 miles (16 to 32 km) from the airport at Martha's Vineyard, but if the plane continued its descent it would hit water before ever reaching land. The first sign of serious trouble appeared at 9:39 P.M. as radar records indicate that Kennedy made a right turn when he should have made a left in preparing to land. He also climbed to an altitude of 2,600 feet (792 m). Kennedy may have been trying to find a way out of the haze, or perhaps he simply lost his bearings.

The craft remained at 2,600 feet for about a minute before making a second right turn and beginning a rapid descent. An experienced corporate pilot for Dewair Inc. described how a pilot can become disoriented under these conditions: "You think the airplane is doing something it's not. You think the plane is turning right, but it's turning left. It only takes a few seconds to put the airplane on a 60-degree angle and into a spin."[10]

That might have happened to JFK Jr. In any case, radar indicates that at 9:40:20 P.M. the plane plummeted to 2,200 feet (670 m) and continued to drop at a rate of 5,000 feet (1,524 m) per minute. That is ten times faster than the average rate of descent. Kennedy's last-minute maneuvers suggest that the plane's autopilot wasn't on. The final radar contact with the aircraft at 9:40:34 revealed that it had fallen to an altitude of 1,100 feet (335 m).

In all likelihood, Kennedy's plane was caught in a rapid and terrifying spin toward the sea known as the graveyard spiral. As a still somewhat inexperienced pilot, Kennedy may have instinctually pulled back on the controls in an effort to lift the plane's nose and stop the drop. But for this to succeed the plane's wings must be level, and this would have been extremely difficult for a pilot without an instrument rating to accomplish under the prevailing conditions. Unless the wings were level, this maneuver would tighten the dive, quickening the plunge into the sea.

Mercifully for those on board, the realization of what was happening would have lasted only about 30 seconds. Death was instantaneous for them. Descending at that speed, the impact would have been similar to hitting a concrete runway.

One puzzling factor was that Kennedy never used his radio to call for help. "As soon as he had an inkling that something was wrong he should have been on the radio," said chief flight instructor Paul Falzarano at Executive Flyers Aviation in Bedford, Massachusetts. "There was a multitude of people he could have called to extricate him from trouble."[11] Why Kennedy never called for help remains an unanswered question. But it's been suggested that it may have all happened too fast, or perhaps the surrounding darkness disoriented Kennedy, who didn't realize what was happening until it was too late.

$\mathcal{M}$eanwhile, at the Kennedy compound in Hyannis Port, John's relatives had gathered for his cousin Rory's bridal dinner. It was a relaxing summer evening filled with good food and laughter. "They were having a great time," a family friend recalled. "They made a quilt for Rory and Mark [her fiancé] and everyone made a square with a footprint or handprint or something representing them."[12] Earlier that day the bride-to-be had gone sailing with her mother, Ethel Kennedy, who was John's aunt. Now the family eagerly looked forward to the Saturday wedding. The white canvas tents for the outdoor reception were already up, and the weather promised to be perfect.

John's plane was not scheduled to arrive until about ten o'clock that evening, so no one at the dinner was concerned about the pair. But that changed when John and Carolyn failed to appear later on. There were inquiry calls, and when the couple did not arrive by two o'clock in the morning, they were officially reported missing. Less than an hour later, the search was under way. The FAA (Federal Aviation Administration) began by checking airports along the way. By 7:30 A.M., once the sun was up, a massive search effort was launched involving fifteen Civil Air Patrol planes, two helicopters, one of which was an Air National Guard chopper, and other search aircraft.

In the water, Coast Guard cutters as well as utility and patrol boats combed the area from Long Island Sound to Cape Cod Bay. They were aided in the hunt by numerous search-and-rescue vessels. Early that morning, President Bill Clinton had been alerted to the situation and offered encouragement and assistance both to John's sister, Caroline Kennedy Schlossberg, and their uncle Senator Ted Kennedy. The president asked to be kept abreast of the progress of the search and told White House Chief of Staff John Podesta, "Let's make sure we are doing everything we can to find them."[13]

Caroline and her husband, Ed Schlossberg, were not at the Kennedy's Hyannis Port compound that evening. They had been celebrating their thirteenth wedding anniversary on a rafting vacation with their children in Stanley, Idaho, when a call came at 4:30 A.M. informing them that John's plane was missing. They flew back to their home in Sagaponack, New York, to wait for further word. They were met there by Caroline's uncle Senator Ted Kennedy, who had come down from Hyannis Port to comfort them. To distract Caroline's children, the senator even played basketball with them.

The mood at the Hyannis Port compound had dramatically shifted as the Kennedy family hoped for the best and braced for the worst. Rory Kennedy's wedding was indefinitely postponed, and the priests there to conduct the ceremony held a mass on the front porch to pray for the safe return of the missing couple. Others living in the vicinity tied yellow ribbons around trees and telephone poles as a symbol of their hope that John and his wife would be rescued. Slowly the caterers and others hired for the wedding vacated the premises. At about 8:30 A.M. guests were called and told not to come. "We were thinking today would be the fun part of living next door to the Kennedys," one neighbor had commented in anticipation of the wedding.[14] But as the hours passed with no sign of John's plane, that was hardly the case.

While word of the missing plane would affect people worldwide, those in Martha's Vineyard and the rest of Cape Cod felt particularly involved. That summer John and his wife had been to Martha's Vineyard nearly every weekend. They stayed at the 375-acre (152-hectare) estate that John and his sister inherited in 1994 following their mother's death. John was a familiar figure on the island, who was often spotted rollerblading or biking along its narrow roadways.

Concern for those on the missing plane, however, was far broader than just the island's population. The nation had become embroiled in the ocean search as millions of Americans watched television reports, hoping for some encouraging news. Outside John and Carolyn's New York apartment building, thousands waited in line for as long as three hours just to leave a note or flowers at the couple's doorstep. At Arlington National Cemetery people laid flowers on President Kennedy's grave and softly prayed for the safe return of his son. President Clinton perhaps best summed up what the nation was feeling when he issued the following statement:

> As the search continues I want to express our family's support and offer our prayers and those of all Americans for John Kennedy Jr., his wife, Carolyn, her sister Lauren, and to their fine families. For more than forty years now, the Kennedy family has inspired Americans to public service, strengthened our faith in the future, and moved our nation forward. Through it all they suffered much and given more."[15]

While the prayers and well-wishes of millions were now focused on the missing trio, as the hours passed hope began to fade. Two types of helicopters had been airborne during the nighttime search. One, outfitted with night-vision capability, allowed the pilot to see in the dark; the other had an infrared capability that permitted the pilot to detect temperature differences in the water. A person alive in the sea would register a higher temperature than his or her surroundings and show up as a different color in the water. But even the latest technology could not alter the reality that there were no signs of survivors anywhere.

There were also growing hints that the worst had occurred. Shortly before noon on Saturday a black overnight case was spotted on the surf near the shore. Damon Seligson, a vacationer on Cape Cod, retrieved it from the water. "I just had an awful feeling in my stomach," he said in describing how he felt as he waded out to get it.[16] He saw a business card in the clear plastic outside pocket, which read "Lauren G. Bessette, Morgan Stanley Dean Witter, Vice President," and immediately knew that Kennedy's plane had crashed. Other telltale articles soon appeared in the water, including a black cosmetic bag with a prescription bottle for Carolyn Kennedy, an aqua duffel bag reportedly belonging to JFK Jr., and carpeting and a headrest from the plane.

The exhaustive search for survivors continued, but it was becoming doubtful that anyone could still be alive in the 68-degree (20-degree C) waters off Cape Cod. Late Sunday night, the Coast Guard switched their efforts from a "search and rescue" to a "search and recovery" mission— acknowledging that there was no longer any hope of finding survivors.

The flag at the Hyannis Port compound was lowered to half-staff, and Senator Kennedy issued a statement describing his family as "filled with unspeakable grief and sadness." A spokesperson for the Bessettes said: "John and Carolyn were true soulmates…we take solace in the thought that together they will comfort Lauren for eternity."[17]

Headlines around the world reported that America's prince had been killed as people everywhere mourned the loss of "our nation's son," whose potential had seemed both endless and magical. The John F. Kennedy Library and Museum in Boston extended its evening hours to allow thousands of visitors to sign the condolence book in the building's lobby. More than 3,000 people visited the library in the days following the fatal accident, and their messages of hope and sorrow filled eleven volumes.

Meanwhile, the recovery effort continued through Tuesday and the start of Wednesday. Confirmation of the inevitable came early Wednesday, July 21. Parts of Kennedy's plane and the bodies of those on board were found beneath 116 feet (35 m) of water. They were about 7 miles (11 km) off the coast of Martha's Vineyard. Senator Ted Kennedy and his two sons, Teddy Jr. and Patrick, a congressman, faced the grim task of being aboard the salvage ship as the bodies were retrieved from the water.

Deciding on an appropriate funeral service for John and his wife was an important issue for the Kennedys. Senator Kennedy favored a large somewhat public service for his nephew. It was rumored that he was trying to obtain special permission for John to be buried with his parents in Arlington National Cemetery. However, John's sister, Caroline, felt differently. Caroline, who placed a high premium on the family's privacy, insisted that there be no public ceremony. After consulting with the Bessette family, it was determined that John, Carolyn, and Lauren would be cremated and their ashes scattered at sea. Prior to his death, JFK Jr. had expressed a desire to be buried at sea. There was another advantage to not having a cemetery plot: The grave could not be turned into a tourist attraction by the curious.

The burial at sea was held on Thursday morning, July 22. Seventeen relatives boarded the Navy destroyer *Briscoe* for the service. At the family's request, the press helicopters were held at bay. They remained at least 10 miles (16 km) from where the service was conducted. Nevertheless, it was impossible for mourners to completely escape the gaze of onlookers. A crowd of tourists and locals gathered to watch the destroyer as it made its way down Vineyard Sound.

On the *Briscoe*, a band played the "Navy Hymn" and Rear Admiral Barry Black, the Navy's deputy chief of chaplains, spoke. One of the officers carried the three ash-filled urns to a small platform from which family members

The Kennedy compound at Hyannis Port,
Massachusetts, has been the setting for many of the family's
joys and sorrows. It was here in November 1960 that John F.
Kennedy awaited election returns, and learned that he would be
president of the United States. Three years later the compound's
flag flew at half-mast after JFK's assassination. In July 1999,
the flag was lowered again—this time for the president's son.

John F. Kennedy had been a Navy hero during World War II,
so it was fitting that his son should be buried at sea. Here family members,
stunned by grief, are aboard a Navy vessel enroute to the private ceremony.
John's cousin Maria Shriver is at far left; Caroline is in the center; Edward
Kennedy is at right. The press complied with Caroline's request that they stay
behind the range of telephoto lenses during the scattering of ashes.

spread their loved ones' ashes over the sea. Red, yellow, and white floral wreaths were tossed into the ocean as the ship left the area.

The following day a memorial service was held at the Church of St. Thomas More. It was the church that John and Caroline had often attended with their mother. Ted Kennedy and his sister Eunice (Caroline's aunt) had initially thought of having the service at St. Patrick's Cathedral in New York City. It is considerably larger and could accommodate more people. But again Caroline chose a more private ceremony.

Three hundred and fifty mourners attended the invitation-only service. These included a large number of family members and longtime political friends. President Clinton, who was there with his wife and daughter, presented the Kennedy and Bessette families with photo albums of John and Carolyn on their 1998 visit to the White House. During the service, Caroline read eleven lines from Shakespeare's play *The Tempest*, which John had been in at college. She had asked her uncle, Ted Kennedy, to say the eulogy. In remembering his nephew, the senator said: "He was lost on that troubled night, but we will always wake for him, so that his time, which was not doubled, but cut in half, will live forever in our memory, and in our beguiled and broken hearts."[18]

Many left the church in tears. Mourners hugged one another seeking comfort and support. Following the service, Caroline Kennedy and her family stepped into a waiting limousine and rode off. A far more private person than her brother was, she generally shunned crowds. Yet today as the somber individuals lining the streets waved to her, a damp-eyed Caroline rolled down the car's window and waved back. It was an unspoken recognition that the country shared her grief.

The Kennedys and John at his christening in December 1960. This was the first photograph of JFK Jr. He would become the subject of countless photos over the next thirty-eight years.

Chapter 2

Prince of the Realm

J ust as the world mourned the death of America's prince, it had rejoiced at his birth thirty-eight years earlier. John Fitzgerald Kennedy Jr. came into the world on November 25, 1960, the day after Thanksgiving. As the first child ever born to a president-elect, he was immediately seen as a gift to be thankful for. Although the Kennedys had a three-year-old daughter named Caroline, they wanted more children. Jacqueline Kennedy, the nation's stylish soon-to-be First Lady, had already had a miscarriage and a stillbirth, and now the country hoped that everything would go well for the family that was considered the American ideal.

John Jr.'s birth was the answer to their prayers. The baby arrived seventeen days early by Cesarean section, which meant that he would spend the first few days of his life in an incubator. Yet he was basically healthy despite a mild lung ailment. Toys, baby clothes, flowers, and well wishes arrived from near and far. There were expensive floral arrangements from such celebrities as the singer-actor Frank Sinatra, and even Queen Elizabeth sent her congratulations. The *London Times* summed up the effect of young John's birth as follows: "Press coverage of the event has been so enthusiastic that one could get the impression that this was a royal birth and the dynasty had been saved."[1]

John's father, the president-elect, beamed with delight the moment he saw his son and joked that he was thinking about naming the baby Abraham Lincoln. Clearly everyone had high expectations for this 6-pound 3-ounce (3-kg) newborn. John Jr. was the latest addition to a very special family. At the age of forty-three, John F. Kennedy was the youngest man ever elected to the presidency. In many ways, he had been the "golden" candidate. Possessing good looks, intelligence, and charm, he had also been blessed with wealth and privilege.

The president-elect was the second-oldest son in an affluent Irish Catholic family headed by his strong-willed father, Joseph P. Kennedy. The elder Kennedy, a self-made millionaire who amassed a sizable fortune, was known for his vigor and unquenchable ambition. He had gone out of his way to instill a keen sense of drive and competitiveness in his brood of nine children. From the time they were able to walk and talk, Kennedy kids were taught the importance of winning. Early on, Joe Kennedy had become acutely aware of the value of image and was frequently known to put façade above reality. He is quoted as once having said, "It's not what you are that counts, but what people think you are," and he diligently strove to convey this to his offspring and their spouses.[2] It would prove vital in shaping the public's perception of his son's presidency.

After Joseph P. Kennedy's eldest son and namesake, Joe, died a hero in a World War II air mission, he focused on John (usually called Jack) to lead the Kennedys into politics. Jack was also a World War II hero, who rescued his crewmates when a Japanese destroyer attacked his torpedo boat, *PT 109*. After the war, Jack served in Congress and then as a senator from Massachusetts. Jack's natural ability coupled with his father's money and connections made for a powerful and desirable presidential candidate.

Jack's wife, Jacqueline Bouvier Kennedy, was an asset to her husband as well. A former debutante of French ancestry on her father's side, Jackie was considered the essence of breeding and refinement. She spoke a number of languages and, during her husband's campaign, made a point of addressing various ethnic groups in their native tongues. Jackie was always a hit at public events, and America couldn't seem to get enough of her. At just thirty-one years of age, this young woman was unlike previous more matronly First Ladies. Known for her glamour and elegance, she became an instant trendsetter. Perhaps the famous photographer Jacques Lowe, who took numerous pictures of the First Family, captured the essence of Jacqueline Kennedy when he said: "She had been called the world's most beautiful woman…yet she wasn't a perfect beauty.…It was her inner beauty and strength, her near royal bearing, her quiet intelligence that people saw and reacted to, that made her the near mythical figure she has become in the eyes of the world.…"[3]

Together Jack and Jackie held out the promise of a magical America with limitless potential and equality for all. The president called his program for America the New Frontier, and through it the Peace Corps was created and Americans set their sights on landing on the moon. President Kennedy told Americans: "Ask not what your country can do for you; ask what you can do for your country," making every citizen a participant in his or her dream for an ideal society.

Much later it was learned that not everything at the White House was as ideal as Washington publicists would have everyone believe. There were the President's extramarital affairs with Hollywood starlets and others and the subsequent emotional distance between husband and wife. Nevertheless, when John Jr. was born they were considered an ideal to emulate, and once their two-month-old son was carried into the White House, John F. Kennedy Jr. became an important part of the dream.

Being the nation's "first son" and growing up in the White House meant an early childhood in the spotlight. Although their mother lamented that John and Caroline lived in an "office building," as she referred to the White House, Jackie did her best to make it feel like home. The family's living quarters were attractively decorated, and while the First Lady hosted a televised tour showing how she had restored various portions of the White House, she firmly insisted that their living area remain private.

When a photo of young John's blue-and-white bedroom was considered for inclusion in the White House Guide Book, Mrs. Kennedy stood firm in her refusal. "Even at the age of two, one's bedroom should be private," she argued.[4] Nevertheless, continually safeguarding her family's privacy became one of the most trying aspects of Jacqueline Kennedy's life since it was actually a nearly impossible feat.

Jacqueline Kennedy wanted John and Caroline to have as normal a childhood as possible, and she went to great lengths to achieve this. Although they occupied arguably one of the nation's most palatial residences, the children were allowed to have a wide assortment of pets to love and play with. In residence at the White House at various times

Caroline adored her baby brother the moment she laid eyes
on him, and the two would remain unusually close throughout John's life. Only they
understood what it was like to be the children of a martyred president, the fixation of
a Kennedy-obsessed public, and the quarry of an insatiable media.

were several dogs, a rabbit, and the youngsters' ponies. Jacqueline Kennedy was an accomplished horsewoman and made certain that her children were on horseback as toddlers. Caroline adored her pony, Macaroni, and rode quite well even as a very young child. John's experience, however, differed. He proved to be allergic to horses and never shared his mother's enthusiasm for equestrian sports. When John was placed on his pony, Leprechaun, for the first time, he immediately asked to be taken off.

While a menagerie of animals seemed to come and go at the White House, these often cuddly creatures meant a great deal to the Kennedy children. John would later cite one of the pets as among his White House memories. "We had a dog who was named Pushinka," he recalled, "who was given to my father by the premier of Russia, the Soviet Union at the time, and it was the daughter of the first dog in space. And we trained it to slide down this slide that we had in the back of the White House, and…sliding the dog down the slide is probably my first memory."[5]

Jacqueline Kennedy was so determined that her children experience normal life that she even established a White House nursery school so that Caroline and eventually John could learn in a typical school environment. The other students attending were the children of White House staffers. Mrs. Kennedy had other help in educating and caring for the children as well. Their British nanny, Maud Shaw, was important to both Kennedy children. When Caroline was in school, it was frequently Shaw who delighted and entertained John.

Maud Shaw had come into John's life during his infancy, and she took tremendous pride in him as he grew and thrived. In time John became attached to Shaw, and one evening, when another woman cared for him, he cried for nearly two hours. Maud Shaw was attuned to the little

*E*ven at the age of three, John F. Kennedy Jr. was irresistible.
*Here he turns on the charm for his nanny, Maud Shaw. Within weeks, John
would ask Shaw if his daddy had taken "a big plane" to heaven.*

boy's needs and dreams, and sometimes she seemed better able to understand him than did his own father. This became evident after President Kennedy, concerned that his son wasn't talking yet, asked Shaw when she thought John would start to speak. "Oh, but he does talk, Mr. President," the nanny earnestly replied, "it's just that you can't understand him." "That's right, Daddy," John's sister, Caroline, chimed in. "He does talk to me." "[Then] I guess you'd better interpret for me," the President jokingly told his daughter.[6]

$\mathcal{D}$espite President Kennedy's difficulty understanding his son's speech, this leader of the free world took time to enjoy his children and afford them an unusual degree of access to him. During summer vacations in Hyannis Port and winter ones at the Kennedy family's Palm Beach home, the President and John especially enjoyed sailing together on the presidential yacht the *Honey Fitz* (Honey Fitz was the nickname of John's great-grandfather John Fitzgerald). Their love of the sea was part of the special bond that had begun to develop between the President and his young son. While Jackie and Caroline might choose to ride or groom their horses, JFK and his namesake preferred to take to the ocean.

John Jr. was proud of having learned to swim and boasted about this to his nanny and others. Often the child's daring and sense of adventure became particularly evident when he approached a swimming pool. "I remember when he was about two years old," noted Jacqueline Kennedy's half-brother Jamie Auchincloss, "not just going off the diving board and into the deep end of the swimming pool at Bailey's Beach in Newport, whether or not there was somebody right there to catch him. But actually asking for help to climb to the high diving board and just racing off the board to 10 feet (3 m) of free fall. His father was always there to catch him."[7] Not unexpectedly, John's love of the water never lessened, and throughout his life he enjoyed an array of seaside sports.

Since early childhood John had also been fascinated by airplanes and helicopters and loved watching the choppers take off and land near the White House lawn. Sitting on his father's lap at the controls of the White House helicopter, he enjoyed pretending that he was the pilot. There would also be spur-of-the-moment rides for the appealing toddler, who upon seeing his father about to take off in the chopper would cling to him begging not to be left behind. On many occasions the President would relent, allowing John to fly in the helicopter with him to Andrews Air Force Base. After the President disembarked, a Secret Service agent would accompany the child on the flight back.

John's devotion to his father was apparent, but his keen fascination with any kind of flying machine did not escape the President. As John Jr.'s uncle Senator Ted Kennedy later related:

> A famous photograph showed John racing across the lawn as his father landed in the White House helicopter and swept up John in his arms. When my brother saw that photo, he exclaimed: "Every mother in the United States is saying, 'Isn't it wonderful to see that love between a son and his father, the way that John races to be with his father.' Little do they know that the son would have raced right by his father to get to that helicopter."[8]

To a great extent President Kennedy also gave his children the run of the White House and the opportunity to drop in on him often. Every morning John and Caroline accompanied their father on his walk to the Oval Office where the President's secretary, Evelyn Lincoln, stood ready with a piece of candy for each of them. The President also kept small model airplanes in his bedroom so he could give them to John on these morning visits. The children would remain there playing with their father for about ten minutes before Maud Shaw arrived on the scene to escort them back to the White House living quarters.

On days when Caroline was momentarily due at nursery school, John was allowed to linger a bit longer and play behind a secret panel in his father's desk that opened like a small door. There are numerous stories of how President Kennedy might be discussing matters of state with cabinet members or foreign dignitaries when John would unexpectedly pop out from beneath his father's desk.

On one such occasion President Kennedy was discussing the British Labour party with Randolph Churchill, when young John jumped out of the desk and gleefully announced, "I'm a big bear and I'm hungry." Determined not to disappoint the boy, the President instantly responded saying, "And I'm a great big bear and I'm going to eat you up in one bite!" Seeing Churchill's surprised expression, Jack Kennedy remarked: "You may think this is strange behavior in the office of the President of the United States, but in addition to being the President, I also happen to be a father."[9]

Americans enjoyed hearing about the adorable toddler in the White House, and reporters anxious to fill this need sometimes got their facts wrong. For years the public thought that John's nickname was John-John, although he was actually never called that by his parents or anyone else in the White House for that matter. A reporter mistakenly thought John's father called him John-John after he heard the President say his son's name twice to capture the busy toddler's attention.

$\mathcal{P}$resident Kennedy strove to be a vital force in his children's lives, but for the most part it was their mother who went to great lengths to constructively mold their personalities. Despite the many demands on her time, Jacqueline Kennedy made raising her children a top priority. "If Caroline and John turn out badly," she said in 1961, "nothing I do in the public eye would have any meaning."[10] When asked what she most wanted to accomplish during the second half of her husband's term in office, the First Lady immediately responded: "More time with my children, for they are both at an age when it is important that their parents be with them as much as possible."[11] She was true to her word. During the first year of the White House nursery school, the students' mothers took turns teaching the class, and Jackie was no exception.

While her glamorous image might lead one to think otherwise, caring for John and Caroline was what Mrs. Kennedy did best. J. B. West, the former chief usher at the White House, observed:

> Many times...I watched her play with [her children] exactly as a child plays....I feel strongly that this was the real Jacqueline Kennedy. She was so happy, so abandoned, so like a little girl who had never grown up. Many times, when she was performing with such grace and authority the role of First Lady, I felt she was just pretending. "She really longs for a child's world," I thought, "where she can run and jump and ride horses."[12]

Well aware that her children were afforded many luxuries, Mrs. Kennedy did not want the "First Family children" to lose touch with what a more typical childhood was like. "I think it's hard enough to bring up children anyway," she once said, "and everyone knows that the limelight is the worst thing for them. They either get conceited or else they get hurt....They need their mother's affection and guidance....That is what gives them security in an often confusing new world."[13] To provide John and his sister with a sense of everyday life, Jackie took them to shopping malls, parks, and other places that children frequented. On Halloween she took the pair trick-or-treating.

When John was born countless baby gifts had come in, and after the family moved to the White House, scores of presents for both children continued to arrive. Believing that no child receiving a daily truckload of toys could remain unspoiled, Jackie had many of the presents sent back. Mrs. Kennedy expressed her concern over this issue when she confided to a friend: "The world is pouring terrible adoration at the feet of my children and I fear for them. How can I bring them up normally?"[14]

John and his sister were encouraged to make rather than buy the presents they gave, and their mother tried to teach them that thoughtfulness and decency were worth more than elaborate displays of wealth. Susan Neuberger Wilson, the mother of one of Caroline's playmates, was impressed with the First Lady's parenting skills. "I was always struck by her calmness and how clearly and simply she spoke to the children in this soft voice," Wilson recalled. "She would say to me, 'I want John and Caroline to grow up to be good people.' That was really her goal."[15]

Although the President often gave in to his children's whims and demands, Mrs. Kennedy insisted on establishing family rules and adhering to them. She was strict about bedtimes and seeing that the children learned to respect the property and feelings of others. To ensure that her child-rearing dictates were adhered to, she sent specific memos to the Secret Service detailing her instructions. One memo read: "If Mrs. Kennedy herself is driving the children, she insists that the follow-up car not be seen by the children." Another stated: "Mrs. Kennedy is adamant that agents must not perform special favors for [John and Caroline] or wait upon them as servants. Agents are not to carry clothes, beach articles [or] sand buckets...for Caroline and John Jr." Mrs. Kennedy also instructed the Secret Service not to accompany them when she took the children water skiing. "Drowning is my responsibility," she assured them.[16]

The differences in the parenting philosophies of the President and the First Lady became obvious to those surrounding the family, including White House staff and even members of Congress. Former Senator George Smathers of Florida, a close friend of the President, noted:

> Jackie was so adamant about not spoiling John, but Jack wanted to spoil him to death....While Jackie tried to keep him under control, Jack would let John break into meetings, interrupt his schedule, and give him whatever he wanted. Jack adored him, thought he was perfect, and wanted to be with him all the time.[17]

The President and First Lady also sharply disagreed on allowing photographs of the children to be shown to the public. The President saw the political value of releasing photos of the adorable White House preschoolers to the press and, as his secretary Evelyn Lincoln put it, felt "that the whole world should be allowed to enjoy his kids within limits." Jackie, on the other hand, did not want John and Caroline to be easy targets for the press. She had told Princess Grace of Monaco: "I'm determined that Caroline and John should be able to get in and out of the White

House without being pestered by photographers or being made constantly aware of their position."[18]

Following John's first birthday, the White House released an official photograph of him to the press, but the media felt cheated. The UPI news service sent a sharply worded letter to the White House press secretary Pierre Salinger, stating:

> Needless to say, we are quite disappointed that we cannot take our own birthday pictures of Baby Kennedy, and that all we will get will be one black and white which the White House will distribute. Can we get at least two different shots—one for the A.M. papers and a different one for the afternoons? Also is there no chance that color pictures could be made for distribution at the same time?[19]

The divergent viewpoints of the President and his wife sometimes placed Salinger in a difficult position. It was nearly impossible for him to prevent enterprising photographers from taking pictures of the children from a distance if they used a telescopic lens. Yet Jackie demanded that no unauthorized photographs of her children be taken and wrote some strongly worded memos to the press secretary on the subject. In one she stated:

> I thought you had made an arrangement with the fotogs not to take the children playing at the WH [White House]. They have had all the pictures of Macaroni [Caroline's pony] they need. I want no more—I mean this—and if you are firm and will take the time, you can stop it. So please do. What is a press secretary for—to help the press, yes—but also to protect us.[20]

"But JFK had another view," Salinger recalled. "When Jackie was away, … he told me now was the time to get wonderful pictures. That's why there are photos now of the kids in his office."[21] At times the President bypassed both his wife and the press secretary and initiated memorable photo sessions on his own. Once when Jackie was away, President Kennedy personally called *Look* magazine photographer Stanley Tretick to invite him to the White House to take some candid photos of John and Caroline.

"I was surprised to get the call," Tretick had said. "I knew that Jackie had been against me taking her kids' pictures…but Jack was getting ready for the presidential campaign [for a second term] and he felt differently. He knew the value of *Look*."[22]

"Things get kind of sticky around here when Mrs. Kennedy's around," the President told the photographer. "But Mrs. Kennedy is away. So now is the time to do some of those pictures you've been asking for of John and Caroline."[23] The nearly weeklong photo shoot resulted in some wonderful pictures, including the famous one of John playing beneath his father's desk in the Oval Office.

There were all sorts of treats to be had when John played beneath the desk with his dad. "He used to give us chewing gum [but] my mother didn't like us to chew gum," John later recalled. "So we'd go over to the Oval Office at night and he'd feed us from under the desk."[24]

*U*sually, however, Jackie had the final say when it came to matters concerning the children, and the positive effects of her choices were evident when John and Caroline were compared to their Kennedy cousins, especially the large and boisterous family of their uncle Bobby, one of JFK's brothers. Although the children's cousins did not live in the White House, they were still "Kennedy kids" and as

JFK was not only a proud father but a savvy politician. He understood the value of a photograph such as this one of young John peeking out from beneath the presidential desk.

such were afforded many advantages. Yet at times it looked as though they hadn't always benefited from their status in life.

Maud Shaw, John and Caroline's nanny, expressed the feeling when she said: "All the other Kennedy children were allowed to do pretty much as they pleased. What people did not expect, though, was that Caroline and John would be such unspoiled nice kids. There was nothing 'bratty' about them."[25]

Jacqueline Kennedy wanted them to stay that way, and even though the close-knit Kennedy clan were generally together for holidays and special family occasions, she tried hard to keep the others from intruding too deeply in her children's lives.

John and Caroline adored their uncles, Bobby and Teddy Kennedy, who like their father were in politics. Ted Kennedy, a Massachusetts senator during his brother's term in office, became a familiar figure in Congress, while Bobby Kennedy worked in the Justice Department after being appointed U.S. attorney general by his brother the President. He later also served as a New York senator. Both Bobby and Teddy took a personal interest in John and Caroline and enjoyed playing with them, but even here Jackie maintained some distance.

As noted Kennedy biographer Doris Kearns Goodwin observed:

> Jackie understood the importance of creating a family unit apart from the larger Kennedy family. She recognized that the children would get strength from the grandparents and cousins [who eventually numbered 29] and aunts and uncles, but it was growing up with a feeling of belonging to their own small family that would give them stability.[26]

Some felt that Jackie's need to separate her children from the other Kennedys was grounded in her distaste for the rowdy competitive atmosphere that typically prevailed when they all got together. Dinah Bridge, a longtime friend of the family, noted that there were sharp personality differences between Jackie and the other Kennedys:

> She was a rather gentle quiet character, and suddenly to be bowled into the Kennedy family, you really had to do a bit of shouting to keep up. Meals were fun, never dull and never quiet. They'd drink gallons of milk and talk and talk, and you might hear Jackie trying to say something at the end of the table. She hardly ever got it out though. Didn't have a chance.[27]

Jackie Kennedy would forgo the traditional family football games at Hyannis Port to pursue more cultural ventures and never really formed strong bonds with the other Kennedy women. She referred to them as the "rah-rah" girls, and they apparently felt similarly.[28] When she told the family that her name was pronounced "Jaclean," they jokingly noted that it rhymed with "queen."[29] Of course, Jackie never forgot that her son was a Kennedy who had his father's name—the most famous Kennedy of all. Still, she was determined that John not be overshadowed by his heritage and be given enough space to develop his own identity.

Jackie encouraged her own children to be there for one another, and Caroline and John always remained close. The Kennedys had done their best to prepare their daughter for the transition from only child to big sister. Maud Shaw helped Caroline pick out a lovely silver brush-and-comb set as a special gift for the new baby, and the little girl beamed with pride whenever Shaw used it on baby John.

John and Caroline often played together during their years at the White House. They shared a unique position as the nation's "first children" along with a dynamic and complex family heritage.

As might be expected, Caroline at times became exasperated with her little brother, who was often quite mischievous. In a letter to her grandmother Rose Kennedy, she once described John as "a bad squeaky boy who tries to spit in his mother's Coca Cola and who has a very bad temper."[30] Caroline didn't stay peeved at him for very long, though. She later wrote this poem about John:

He paints his bathroom walls in the middle of the night.
He comes into my room and unscrews every light....
I love him not just because I oughter
But also because blood runs thicker than water.[31]

John adored his big sister, and at least one family friend noted that the best way to get John to do something was to have Caroline ask him.

Undeniably, on numerous occasions the White House toddler, whose Secret Service code name was Lark, became the center of attention for all the wrong reasons. Once when the Iranian Empress Farah Diba offered him a flower in the White House garden, he firmly said "no" and refused to accept it. On another occasion a TV camera caught the toddler as he accidentally dropped his toy gun from a balcony just as Marshal Tito, head of state from the former Yugoslavia, was about to deliver a speech. The toy actually landed at the dignitary's feet, though the media reported it as falling on Tito's head.

John loved guns, helmets, and watching the White House events. He was thrilled when visiting generals allowed him to try on their hats, and he diligently practiced saluting. At one point the President feared that his son might become overly entranced with the military and confided to a friend: "I'm concerned about John's fascination with military things. He's right there whenever he sees guns, swords or anyone wearing a uniform....I guess we all go through that phase. John just sees more of the real thing."[32] As it turned out, John never enlisted in the service as an adult, and at the White House, Maud Shaw usually managed to keep the young soldier's behavior in check. She would encourage him to act like a "big boy"—a status that John was extremely eager to attain.

It looked as if John Fitzgerald Kennedy Jr. might grow up as a middle child once it became known at the White House that Jacqueline Kennedy was expecting another baby. But on August 7, 1963, while eight months pregnant and vacationing at Cape Cod, the First Lady began experiencing severe pain. Mrs. Kennedy along with her obstetrician, who was on call in Cape Cod, and several Secret Service agents quickly took a helicopter to the nearby Otis Air Force Base hospital. Though Jackie had planned to have the child at Walter Reed Hospital in Washington, D.C., there was no time for that now.

After being notified, the President immediately left the White House to fly to his wife's side. By the time he arrived Jackie had given birth to a baby boy they named Patrick Bouvier Kennedy. The premature infant, however, only weighed 4 pounds 10 ounces (2 kg) and suffered from a lung ailment similar to what John had as an infant. Sadly, Patrick's health problems were much more severe.

Realizing that the tiny boy's difficulty breathing meant his survival was at stake, the baby was flown to a large well-equipped hospital. Despite the efforts of the staff there, Patrick lost his fight for life in the early hours of August 9, 1963. The child's death took a heavy toll on

John's parents. They were both already in love with this baby and the loss was shattering.

John was told that his little brother went to live in heaven with God, but it's doubtful that the small child fully understood what happened. Yet within months John would have to deal with another loss that would devastatingly affect the rest of his life.

*I*n November 1963 shortly before John's third birthday, the President was planning a trip to Texas as part of his reelection campaign. For an added touch of glamour Jackie was to accompany him, making this her first political tour since her husband's 1960 presidential campaign. Vice President Lyndon B. Johnson and his wife came along too. Things went pretty well in Fort Worth, and everyone in the presidential party hoped it would continue that way at their next stop in Dallas.

The President was to speak at a luncheon at the Dallas Trade Mart on November 22. He would arrive there in a motorcade that passed through the city's streets. Kennedy sat in the back of an open limousine with Jackie to his left. Texas Governor John B. Connally sat in front of Kennedy with his wife at his side as well. Secret Service agents followed in a limousine behind the President's. Vice President and Mrs. Johnson rode in the third car of the motorcade.

Secret Service agents were in the crowd as well as in the motorcade. A strong core of Kennedy opposition existed in Dallas, and the President had received death threats. Nevertheless, things appeared to be going well at first. The crowd in the streets cheered and waved to Kennedy as his car passed. Then suddenly at 12:30 P.M. three shots rang out from the sixth-floor window of a building along the route. President Kennedy was hit in the head and neck, while Governor Connally was shot in the back.

The injured men were rushed to a nearby hospital. Governor Connally recovered, but the President never regained consciousness. Though the doctors tried hard to save him, John Fitzgerald Kennedy was pronounced dead at 1:00 P.M. His alleged assassin, a man named Lee Harvey Oswald, was later apprehended.

Jackie was still in Dallas but she wanted her children to know what happened before they heard it from an outside source. Maud Shaw broke the news to Caroline, and Jackie had the children's uncle Bobby Kennedy tell John. Days later the Kennedy children stood at their mother's side as their father's funeral procession passed. John bravely saluted his father's casket, creating a heartbreaking image that would be permanently etched in the hearts and minds of Americans throughout the country. Sadly, the funeral had taken place on the boy's third birthday.

Despite the tragedy that shook the nation and most deeply affected her own family, Jacqueline Kennedy had the presence of mind to do what she could to ensure her husband's place in history. She was determined not to let historians—those "bitter old men," as she referred to them—draft the public's eventual impression of the Kennedy administration.[33] Jackie was adamant that JFK be known as a president who tried to create a society as shining and perfect as a legendary mythical kingdom.

She invited journalist and presidential biographer Theodore H. White to Hyannis Port to tell him what she believed Americans needed to remember when they thought about the slain president. "Jack's life had more to do with myth, legend, saga, and story," Mrs. Kennedy told White, "than with political theory or political science....When Jack quoted anything, it was usually classical, but I'm so ashamed of myself—all I keep thinking of is this line from a musical comedy [*Camelot*]: 'Don't let it be

One of the most poignant, painful moments
in American history: Three-year-old John F. Kennedy Jr.
salutes as his father's casket passes by.

forgot/ That once there was a spot/ For one brief shining moment/ That was known as Camelot.' There'll be great presidents again—and the Johnsons [the former Vice President and his wife] are wonderful, they've been wonderful to me—but there'll never be another Camelot."[34]

If JFK was Camelot's king, then young John was its prince. The little boy became heir to the idealistic view the public had of his father, and many would have the same expectations for him. As John grew, scores of Americans wished that he would one day enter politics and bring back Camelot.

In the days following his father's death, however, those around John were more concerned with the boy's immediate future. It was difficult to know the full effect of the funeral on such a young child. Apparently, even seeing his father's casket did not make the finality of death real for the little boy. Maud Shaw tried to help John understand by telling him, "Your father has gone to heaven to look after Patrick." John, thinking his father might have gone there on *Air Force One* replied, "Did he take the big plane with him? I wonder when he's coming back."[35]

Chapter 3

A Different Life

L eaving the White House was difficult for both the First Family and the loyal staff that served them. John's mother did her best to maintain her composure in public during the day, as presidential biographer Theodore White noted: "She had performed flawlessly, superbly. I know now she wanted to cry and she could not."[1] At night in the privacy of her room, though, the former First Lady sobbed bitterly over the loss of her husband. Now she faced the daunting task of raising her children alone, and despite the support of friends and family, at times the future seemed overwhelming.

Being so young and not fully comprehending what had occurred made things especially hard for John. He became hysterical as he watched his toys and beloved stuffed animals packed for the move. The little boy felt certain he would never see his treasures again. Maud Shaw did her best to calm him, allowing John to keep some of his favorite things with him. Nevertheless, his nanny couldn't change the fact that John was about to leave the White House. The only home he had ever known and felt comfortable in would no longer be part of his life.

At times young John's glimpses into the reality of his predicament became painfully clear. This happened one afternoon when a Secret Service agent took John for one of his last walks outside the White House. "I was getting him a drink out of the fountain," the agent recalled, "and a photographer came up and took some pictures. John looked him right in the eye and said, 'What are you taking my picture for? My Daddy's dead.' The poor photographer started to cry. I cried too."[2]

Despite her personal grief, Jackie knew she had to keep things together for John and Caroline's sake. Initially, she and the children stayed with some family friends before purchasing a house in Washington, D.C., close to where she and her husband had lived before JFK was elected president. If creating a normal environment for her children was important to Mrs. Kennedy in the White House, it became her overriding concern as a single parent. White House press secretary Pierre Salinger said that just two days after the assassination she had told him:

> Pierre, there is only one thing I can do now. I have to take care of those kids day by day. I have to make sure they become intelligent. I have to make sure they do good work in school. I have to make sure when they get older that they have strong views on what they should be doing. This is the only thing I can do anymore.[3]

It was during this period that John's uncles, Bobby and Teddy Kennedy, did their best to fill the void in the children's lives left by JFK's death. To young John's delight, Bobby sometimes took him to work with him at the Justice Department. Regardless of his schedule, Bobby made certain that he and John had some time to play together nearly every day, and John was known to giggle gleefully whenever he thought he outsmarted his uncle at hide-and-seek. Both Caroline and John spent more time those days at Hickory Hill, Bobby's country home in Virginia. There they played for hours with their cousins, feeling solidly part of a larger family unit.

Jackie now encouraged John's relationship with Bobby, which she saw as an important tie to her son's heritage. "They think of Hickory Hill as their home," she later said. "Anything that comes up involving a father, like Father's Day at school, I always mention Bobby's name...." In commenting on his uncle's effect on the boy, Jackie added, "Jack made John the mischievous, independent boy he is. Bobby is keeping that alive."[4] Ted Kennedy, JFK's youngest brother, also became a more familiar figure in the boy's life. His uncles' efforts were effective, and as an adult John would say: "Teddy and Bobby—one of the things that they really took a great interest in was the family and the cousins and making a sense of community. It's one of the great, lucky things about being in my family."[5]

Others who were close to the family tried to be there for John as well. Secret Service protection of the President's family did not end with his death, and John was especially fond of Robert Foster, one of the agents assigned to protect them. Foster went out of his way to play with the boy, but when Mrs. Kennedy noticed that her son repeatedly referred to the agent as Daddy, she thought that John might be getting overly attached and requested that Foster be transferred.

Nevertheless, it was obvious to anyone who knew Jackie and the children that they desperately needed the

Secret Service as a barrier from the American public, which still had a keen interest in them. Jackie, now struggling to get on with her life, soon saw that it was impossible to maintain any semblance of privacy in the nation's capital. Local residents, as well as visitors to the capital, wanted to see where the former First Lady and her children lived. Some of them, along with celebrity photographers, would wait outside hoping to catch a glimpse of Jackie or the children. To worsen the situation, sightseeing buses began cruising the street as well.

This predicament made a tense and difficult time for the small family even more stressful. Following her husband's assassination, Jackie feared for her children's lives. If the president of the United States could so easily be murdered, she wondered what assurances there were that John and Caroline would be safe. Tired of living with their shades tightly drawn at all times, Jackie knew that she needed to get John and Caroline out of Washington, D.C.

The answer proved to be a five-bedroom apartment in an exclusive New York City apartment building at 1040 Fifth Avenue. The apartment overlooked Central Park, and it would be John and Caroline's home for many years. Jackie had spent her early childhood in New York, and she and the children had relatives in the city. Jackie's sister Lee and her husband, Stanislas Radziwill, lived just down the street, and Steve and Jean Kennedy Smith (JFK's sister) lived nearby as well. Their son William Kennedy Smith was John's favorite cousin, and now the boys would attend the same school. Jackie hoped that the environment would be better for them in New York City—a large, celebrity-filled town where John and Caroline might be able to escape public scrutiny. Writer Pete Hamill, who became a close friend of Jackie's, described why New York was an ideal place for John to grow up:

I think this city [makes] it possible for a kid who was famous for something he didn't do to have a life. Because the only New Yorkers who care about celebrities are editors and tourists. Nobody would cross the street to ask him [John] for an autograph, they wouldn't do that.[6]

*A*s expected, things went well for the Kennedy trio in New York. Like his cousin William, John was enrolled at St. David's, a small Catholic boys' school where he seemed to fit in well and quickly made friends. Early on, John showed himself to be an energetic youngster who enjoyed tennis and playing soccer with his friends in Central Park. At first both John and Caroline weren't invited to some of their classmates' birthday parties because the other children's parents did not want to look like social climbers cozying up to the Kennedys. Realizing the situation, however, Jackie contacted the other families and urged them to feel free to include her son and daughter. It wasn't long before John and Caroline were regular partygoers. Invitations to the Kennedy children's parties were especially prized. One of John's young classmates recalled:

Jackie had a big notice board in the apartment filled with family snapshots, just like any mother would have. One or two of the children sneaked away with some of the snapshots to take home to their parents afterwards because they wanted souvenirs of their visit to the Kennedys.[7]

In many ways John's life was not much different from that of other upper-class boys in New York City. His mother walked him to school every day (though the Secret Service agents were never far behind), he collected baseball cards, and he invited friends over to play after school. Jackie purchased a ten-room farmhouse in the fashionable community of Bernardsville, New Jersey, so that the children could enjoy the countryside on weekends. There were also wonderful vacations with John's cousins both at the seashore and ski resorts.

While Jackie wanted John to never forget his heritage, she also strongly encouraged him to be his own person. That this was happening became apparent on a ski trip that Jackie and her children took with Bobby Kennedy and his family. John had fallen on the slopes and started crying, when his uncle Bobby approached him saying, "Kennedys don't cry." John looked him straight in the eye and responded, "This Kennedy cries."[8]

In elaborating on how his mother insisted that he forge his own path, years later John would say in an interview:

> I think [Caroline and I] have a strong sense of my father's legacy and how important it is. But at the same time, there is a sense…that things are different and he would have wanted us to go on with our own lives, and not reenact his.[9]

John proved to be an outgoing, fun-loving boy with a flair for comedy. He was known to do a hilarious imitation of The Beatles that always left his mother and sister weak with laughter. As a White House toddler, John was described by his nanny, Maud Shaw, as a "boy and a half," and his seemingly endless energy and exuberance were still with him when he started school. Family members and friends would later tease John about the time he tried to herd ponies through the reception tent at a relative's wedding. Though John, along with his mother and sister, rarely returned to the White House, they accepted an invitation to

Although photographers pursued them everywhere, Jackie was determined that her children would not lead a sheltered life. The three went rowing in Central Park just after their 1964 move to New York City. A year later, five-year-old John joined his Uncle Bobby's family on a skiing vacation in Sun Valley, Idaho.

a private dinner with President Richard Nixon (the president who succeeded Lyndon Johnson) and his family. Caroline jokingly bet her little brother that he wouldn't be able to get through the meal without spilling something. Apparently, Caroline knew him all too well—when John accidentally tipped over his glass of milk into President Nixon's lap, their host reacted graciously.

$\mathcal{J}$ohn was also beginning to acquire the thoughtfulness and charm he would be known for as an adult. Shortly after the White House dinner, John wrote the following thank-you note to the Nixons for their hospitality:

February 4, 1971

Dear Mr. President
Dear Mrs. Nixon

I can never thank you more for showing us the White House....I don't think I could remember much about the White House, but it was really nice seeing it all again. When I sat on Lincoln's bed and wished for something my wish really came true. I wished that I [would] have good luck at school....I really loved the dogs, they were so funny, as soon as I came home my dogs kept on sniffing me. Maybe they remember the White House.[10]

John remained fun-loving as he grew older. Sometimes, he would delight in deliberately slipping away from his Secret Service protectors. On at least one occasion, he was forced to deal with the consequences of such behavior. That day John managed to dodge the agents to go biking in Central Park. However, he didn't ride home, because a thief had made off with his expensive Italian-made bike. Though the

Secret Service agents were embarrassed, Jackie thought it was a valuable lesson on life in the real world.

John's mother believed that learning what life was like for those less fortunate was important in developing a strong sense of social responsibility. Working to build a more equitable and just society was part of the Kennedy legacy, and had been evident in the political goals of John's father and his uncles Bobby and Teddy Kennedy. With their father gone, Jackie was glad that Bobby Kennedy now tried to instill these values in John and his sister.

> I didn't want the children to be just two kids living on Fifth Avenue and going to nice schools.... There's so much else in the world, outside this sanctuary we live in. Bobby has told them about the rats and the terrible living conditions that exist here in the midst of a rich city....Broken windows letting in the cold...John was so touched by what he [Bobby Kennedy] said that he said he'd go to work and use the money he made to put windows in those houses. The children rounded up their best toys last Christmas and gave them away. I want them to know about how the rest of the world lives.[11]

While for the most part John remained in his highly protective environment, there were instances in which reality painfully intruded. His mother witnessed this on the second anniversary of her husband's death while walking her son home from school. A small group of boys behind them had tauntingly called out, "Your father's dead! Your father's dead!" John never lost his composure; instead he quickened his stride to keep up with his mother and firmly clasped her hand. It was as though "he were trying to assure me that things were all right," Jackie said in relating the incident. "Sometimes it almost seems that he is trying to protect me instead of the other way around."[12] John would handle similarly difficult situations equally well throughout his life. As an adult he attributed his attitude to his mother's philosophy, which he described as "a sense of not worrying too much about things you can't control and living your life."[13]

Unfortunately, many painful incidents occurred in John's family that were out of their control. Bobby Kennedy, who had become a vital father figure for John, was running for president in 1968 when he was assassinated by a Jordanian immigrant named Sirhan Sirhan. His death shattered Jackie, who felt that she and her children might never be safe in their own country. After seeing Bobby Kennedy buried in Arlington National Cemetery in a grave near her husband's she said, "If they're killing Kennedys, then my children are targets."[14] Her cousin John H. Davis added, "She was utterly devastated by it [Bobby's assassination]. She wanted to get out of the country at all costs. She almost gave up on America altogether."[15]

The ticket out came in the form of her marriage to the Greek shipping tycoon Aristotle Onassis, who was many years older than Jackie. He was said to be among the richest men in the world. Now something of an international playboy, he had garnered a fortune over the years through shrewd business dealings. Onassis owned the island of Skorpios off the coast of Greece, where Jackie and her children could enjoy the privacy she longed for. Fabulously wealthy, he had the resources to ensure that Jackie and the children were adequately protected. "My sister needs a man like Onassis," Jackie's sibling Lee had said, "who can protect her from the curiosity of the world."[16]

Ted Kennedy helped Jackie arrange a prenuptial agreement through which Onassis would give her $3 million prior to their marriage as well as establish a million-dollar trust fund for John and Caroline. Nevertheless, the Kennedys for the most part were against Jackie's wedding plans. Even John's grandmother Rose Kennedy, who supported Jackie's choice, recalled her surprise at hearing the news:

> I was rather stunned...and then perplexed. I thought of the difference in their ages. I thought of the difference in religion, he being Greek Orthodox, and the fact that he had been divorced; and I wondered whether this could be a valid marriage in the eyes of the church. I thought of Caroline and John Jr. and whether they could learn to accept Onassis in the role of stepfather so that he could give them the guidance that children need from a man.[17]

There was even less enthusiasm coming from the Onassis camp. Aristotle Onassis, who lacked a formal education, liked to surround himself with both celebrities and well-bred individuals. Marrying the former First Lady would afford him the status in society he yearned for. Onassis' children from his first marriage, Alexander and Christina, had for years unrealistically clung to the hope of their parents reconciling and were disappointed though not shocked by their father's plans to marry Jacqueline Kennedy.

"It's a perfect match," his son Alexander stated. "Our father loves [famous] names and Jackie loves money."[18] Indeed, the Onassis children knew well the mean-spirited joke on the tip of everyone's tongue at the time, which went:

John Kennedy: "My mother calls you the frog."
Aristotle Onassis: "Why is that?"
John Kennedy: "Because she says when you croak, we'll be rich!"[19]

A friend of Onassis reported that his children "wept bitter tears" at the wedding and that Alexander had said: "My father needs a wife, but I don't need a stepmother."[20]

*J*ohn felt differently about his stepfather, and in the months ahead the two would get along well. Prior to his mother's marriage to Onassis, it was proposed that Jackie would spend nine months with John and Caroline at the Fifth Avenue apartment while the children were attending school in New York City. Knowing how important Jackie's children were to her, Onassis consented, saying:

> Jackie is often at the other end of the world with her children—whom I should say I love very much...but they need time to get used to me, and I want to give them that time. They need time to understand that their mother has remarried and that I want to be their friend, and not replace their father, whom I admired so much. A father cannot be replaced, especially one like John Kennedy. I only desire that they consider me a best friend. That is another reason why I believe it is a good idea that Jackie has time with her children."[21]

There were, however, still summer and holiday vacations on Skorpios when Jackie and the children were together with Onassis. To try to ensure that the youngsters weren't bored during these periods, their stepfather created a children's paradise. Caroline received a number of exciting

Although Jackie's marriage to Aristotle Onassis
*was complex and uneasy, he was always affectionate and generous
to her children. Here nine-year-old John accompanies his mother
and stepfather on an outing in New York City.*

gifts, while among John's were a mini-jeep, a jukebox, and a speedboat. Just in case the children missed American food, the wealthy shipping magnate had Coney Island hot dogs flown in regularly. The children were each given a Shetland pony. On one occasion an Olympic Airlines pilot even flew John's pet bunny from New York to Greece. In addition, both John and Caroline were allowed to invite any of their friends for vacations either on Skorpios or on Onassis's yacht the *Christina*. One summer John invited his cousin Will Smith as well as Bob Kramer, a friend from school. The three eleven-year-old boys spent most of their time swimming and listening to seafaring stories from the crew.

John grew close to Onassis, though Caroline reportedly failed to. "I liked him," John later said of his stepfather. "Caroline didn't but she was old enough to remember our father.…To me, Onassis was a father. After the first year, I was closer than my mother was to him."[22] John also became fond of Onassis's son, Alexander, who was twelve years older. In some ways Alexander was a sort of hip older brother to John, and though he never cared for Jackie, Alexander wholeheartedly embraced her children. The young man especially liked taking John for speedboat rides and enjoying water sports with him. When Alexander was killed in a plane crash in 1973, John took it hard.

John basically had a good relationship with Alexander's father, but at times the billionaire lost patience with the child. According to one story, Onassis became annoyed with John during a party on his yacht, when the boy refused to stop firing a toy gun at his guests. Supposedly, Onassis grabbed the toy from the boy, tossed it overboard, and sent John to his cabin. Enraged at how her husband handled the situation, Jackie threw Onassis's costly camera into the sea and left the party to comfort her son. Nevertheless, for the most part, John enjoyed the time he spent with his stepfather. There was little that Onassis wouldn't do for John or buy for him. Both John and his stepfather loved the sea, and to please the child, Onassis bought John a small red fishing boat and hired a fisherman to take the boy out in it.

Though his stepfather continued to heap luxuries on him, John never acted like a snob while on Skorpios. According to Onassis's longtime secretary Kiki Moutsatsos, John did not feel that his advantages put him above others and still sought out friendships with people of far lesser means. At times when John was on the Christina, "he liked to eat in the kitchen with the crew," Moutsatsos said. "Any time he could get away from his mother's side, he'd go into the kitchen and sit down with them."[23]

With Jackie as Mrs. Aristotle Onassis, in some ways John had to straddle two worlds. Onassis might have become his stepfather, but Jackie wanted to make sure that her son would never lose touch with his true identity. So in the summer of 1972, Jackie invited her first husband's former press secretary, Pierre Salinger, to sail with them aboard the *Christina*. Jackie hoped that now that John was a little older, Salinger could make his father's memory real for him in a meaningful way. "I want you to spend an hour or an hour and a half with John Jr. and Caroline and explain everything about what their father did," Jackie told Salinger.[24]

Salinger rose to the occasion, providing exciting tales of their father's feats in both World War II and the White House. "The kids were very excited about all the things I told them," he noted, "because they had not had that kind of information about their father. I think they got something important in their brains for the future."[25]

Getting important things into John's brain was sometimes a challenge for Jackie as her son grew older. After attending St. David's, John in 1968 entered the third grade at Collegiate, the oldest private school in New York City, where it became obvious that he was not a gifted scholar. When his mother saw how upset he was about his poor spelling, she would remind him that his father had been a terrible speller but was still elected president. It was later learned that John was both dyslexic and somewhat hyperactive. Though intelligent, having a learning disability meant that he would have to work harder in school, and John wasn't always inclined to do so. For the most part, he remained an average student who was sometimes known to misbehave a bit—including getting into a few fights.

Rather than excelling in the classroom, John found that his true arena was the playing field. He was a natural athlete and did well in a variety of sports. Like many of the other school moms, Jackie was always at games and competitions to encourage him. "She was involved in everything John did," Carol Rosenwald, another Collegiate mother, observed. "She was a wonderful parent."[26] That assessment was shared by John Mosler Sr., also a parent at the school, who noted that "Jackie attended every single Collegiate event..."[27]

John's sharp wit and sense of humor contributed to his popularity. At times, however, he couldn't resist having some fun with the ardent Kennedy watchers who were on the lookout for members of his family. Once a woman approached him near school to ask if John F. Kennedy Jr. was anywhere around. John replied, "I don't see him anywhere at the moment." "Well then what's he really like?" she continued. "He's a nice kid," John replied, "and really really smart."[28]

As a youth and later as an adult, John had the ability to see the humorous side of things, which often helped him to put situations into perspective. When his homework assignment at Collegiate had been to write a play, Kennedy's friend Peter Blauner recalled that John wrote one about a playwright who has difficulty writing. "He was riffing about the various characters he'd tried to create," Blauner said, "from a ballet dancer to a deranged pretzel vendor in Central Park. It was really funny."[29] Ironically, John had a flair for drama, and in 1977, while at Collegiate, he landed a role in the school production of the musical *Oliver!* John enjoyed being in the play and enthusiastically rehearsed the show's musical score at home. Although the young actor was the only celebrity in the play, the other cast members still thought of him as no different from themselves. Peter Cohan, another Collegiate student in the show, explained the atmosphere this way:

> The usual Secret Service agents in gray suits were on guard along with a few photographers, but none of the boys in *Oliver!* made a big deal of being in the play with John or of John himself. To us, John was just another kid from a rich family, like a lot of the other kids at Collegiate. We didn't feel sorry for him or anything like that. He just blended in.[30]

Peter's mother added:

> I saw John and Peter in *Oliver!* two or three times and you wouldn't have picked John out as the most handsome boy. He was just one of the boys. But I do remember that his mother and Caroline came to see *Oliver!* and that Aristotle Onassis and several bodyguards came with them.[31]

His mother insisted that John "experience life," and by his early teens, he was a seasoned globe-trotter who often took exotic trips with members of the Kennedy family. In 1975, John accompanied his aunt and uncle, Eunice and Sargent Shriver, and their son Timothy on a visit to Moscow.

To help John academically, his mother invited a tutor to join her son on the island of Skorpios when school was out. At Collegiate, fifteen-year-old Denis Maduro had given "student-taught" classes in math and creative writing, which John enjoyed. Therefore, when it became clear that John could benefit from private tutoring, Maduro seemed like the ideal candidate for the job. The young teen readily agreed to spend the summer in Greece as John's tutor and companion. It proved to be a wonderful experience filled with learning and fun for both boys. Maduro was treated as a family member. He described John's relationship with his stepfather as "very cordial and friendly," noting that the two enjoyed swimming together.

Aristotle Onassis was known for the fabulous jewelry he gave Jackie, but that summer the boys spent some of their spare time making their own jewelry creation for John's mother. Dennis Maduro described how they went about it:

> We got together on the island of Skorpios to get a special present for her. And we had learned scuba diving there. And we scuba dived for a two-week period for special clams that were on the bottom, which we dried out to create a rainbow effect, attached various unique and precious beautiful shells, and presented this to her on her birthday."[32]

Apparently the gift meant a great deal to the former First Lady. While she sometimes gave away jewelry pieces from Onassis, she never parted with this present. According to Maduro, "this was very special [and] she was actually in tears when she got it."[33]

After his stepfather's death in 1975, John spent less time in Greece. But things had begun to sour between his mother and Aristotle Onassis long before then. Onassis complained about Jackie's extravagance—on one occasion, for example, she had gone to an exclusive shoe store and charged two hundred pairs of shoes amounting to $60,000 to her husband's account.

Jackie, on the other hand, had grown tired of hearing about her husband's extramarital affairs. Despite his marriage to Jackie, Onassis maintained an ongoing and fairly public love relationship with the famous Greek opera singer Maria Callas. Once John become old enough to realize what was happening, his feelings for his stepfather cooled somewhat. Despite his age, John saw himself as his mother's protector and did not appreciate Onassis's open humiliation of her.

At about this time another unsettling incident occurred in John's seemingly ideal life. He was unable to go to camp with one of his school friends after the Federal Bureau of Investigation (FBI) learned that he had become the target of extremists. Not long afterward, members of two fringe groups were arrested for plotting to kidnap John—one with terrorist affiliations was politically opposed to U.S. policies. To them, a former president's son from an "all-American family" made an ideal target.

The situation between John's mother and Aristotle Onassis continued to deteriorate, and there were reports that Onassis had been contemplating divorce near the time of his death. In any case, Jackie, along with John and Caroline, were present for Onassis's funeral on Skorpios, though Jackie reportedly remained dry-eyed through it all. After negotiations, John's mother eventually received more than $26 million from Onassis's estate for herself and her children. For a second time in his life, John was left affluent and fatherless.

Jackie had managed to raise her son to be both idealistic
and unpretentious. What she probably hadn't anticipated was that John
would blossom into a young man who looked like a movie star and who
was constantly pursued by swooning teenage girls.

Chapter 4

Teen Idol?

As John matured, in many ways he seemed like a typical teenager. According to family friend Pete Hamill: "He was a wonderful, big, clumsy, awkward, handsome kid. And like every kid, trying on every other week a new identity, the way some people try on clothes. He had a wonderful sense about him that I liked very much. He never tried to be smarter or hipper than he was, so he had no guile….I think he would sit down, like any kid at sixteen and say, 'Does she love me because of me or because of my name?' You know, I think he would have said those kinds of things. But you didn't see it much."[1]

There was an appealing charm about the teenage John Kennedy, and as Barbara Gibson, Rose Kennedy's secretary, noted, he did not seem to have the aggressiveness characteristic of some of his relatives. This was especially noticeable when John played football with his cousins at Hyannis Port. "Ethel's boys, the Shriver boys, and the Smith boys all had distinctive personalities," Gibson recalled. "But John Jr. just sort of flowed with the group. I never had the impression that he was…competitive."[2] John was decidedly more easygoing and fun to be around, and while at times some of his cousins openly envied his "crown prince status," they couldn't help but like him. "John is a good guy. He's his own man," John's cousin Bobby Kennedy Jr. would later say of him. "He doesn't love the spotlight, but he's not uncomfortable there."[3]

The perception of John as a "good guy" was also noted by Jim Conners, a former Palm Beach police officer, who observed both John and his cousins as they grew older and felt that John outstripped the others in many ways. Conners said:

> Jackie brought out the culture in John and Caroline….They are not like run-of-the-mill Kennedys. Everything is low profile, and they think before they leap. John isn't aggressive or forceful; he is a nice, quiet kid, smooth and easygoing. The other kids have a more "go get em" attitude, while John is sophisticated and extremely polite.[4]

Though many people saw John's inherent goodness shining through, he could hardly be characterized as a teenage model of perfection. Jackie often chuckled at her son's antics, but she had to admit that he sometimes got into trouble. Kennedy biographer Ed Klein described the situation this way: "She [Jackie] absolutely adored him…but she also found him to be a handful."[5]

The summer after Onassis died, when John returned to Skorpios with Jackie, he spent much time with Christos Kartanos, a Greek teenager he had been friends with for years. Kartanos was somewhat awed by John's daring, and the youths spent hours doing some high-speed boating around the island. The pair also did their share of smoking and drinking that summer. John gave Kartanos the money for the alcohol so his mother wouldn't know he was buying it. Kartanos said:

> We spent a lot of time together, smoking and drinking wine and I noticed he [John] developed a taste for Scotch. Whenever I went to see him, I carried the Scotch in a cloth shoulder bag. We used to swig it straight from the bottle. John said it made him feel good. But we never got drunk. I think that all the things John did—like drinking wine and whiskey and smoking Greek cigarettes—were his ways of showing off. It's as if he were saying, "Look, I'm not a kid anymore."[6]

John also found a friend in the United States with whom to express his teen rebellion. It was Wilson McCray, another student at Collegiate, who temporarily became John's "partner in crime." "John and I were in the same class and we were really good friends," McCray said. "We were bad little boys. When we were at Collegiate together, John and I used to run away from the Secret Service together and hang out in Central Park and play Frisbee."[7] Their daring increased while the two fourteen-year-olds were vacationing in Switzerland where they took a car out for a joyride. "We went out and spun it around the ice, drove it around, then drove it back," McCray said in describing the incident. He further claims that at times they also experimented with marijuana. "At school we were always getting caught for getting stoned," he added.[8]

JFK Jr. also smoked pot after he entered Phillips Academy in 1976, a prestigious prep school in Andover, Massachusetts, where many children of the country's rich and famous went. In the 1970s recreational use of marijuana was not uncommon among these young people, and on one occasion John was caught by a campus security guard sharing a joint with his classmates at a party. It was obvious, however, that drugs were not about to become a major factor in John Kennedy's life, and while he might have occasionally slipped from the straight and narrow, such excursions were brief. As Holly Owen, a faculty member, noted:

> John smoked grass, but it didn't appear to affect him. I think that his drug escapade was part of his rite of passage, a light experimentation as part of a group. When John experimented with drugs it was only to be one of the boys, not because he was out of control.[9]

John was still very close to his mother, who remained the guiding force throughout much of his life. After Bobby Kennedy's death, Ted Kennedy also became a more important source of strength for John. Ted worked hard to be certain John knew what his father was and the kind of person he was expected to be as well. As a family friend noted:

> Ted was definitely a father figure to them [John and Caroline], making sure they were brought into his own family's activities....He used to talk to John about his father, about the wonderful things, educate him about his father's values. Teddy has always mattered a great deal to John.[10]

In keeping with the Kennedy tradition of helping those in need, John began doing volunteer work while still a teenager. In June 1976 he and his cousin Timothy Shriver went to Guatemala to help earthquake victims. The boys dug trenches, helped rebuild shattered structures, and gave out food. John did his best to speak Spanish and fit in with the other volunteers. It was obvious that he was there to help—not to be a celebrity. John also tried not to be a celebrity at Phillips Academy, although some students remained in awe of him. There was never a shortage of girls wanting to date him, but the girl that John spent most of his time with was Jenny Christian, the daughter of a Manhattan doctor, whom many regarded as the best-looking girl on campus. At Phillips as at Collegiate, John was not an exceptional student, although he continued to enjoy sports and acting classes. He was in a number of theatrical productions including *Petticoats and Union Suits*, *A Comedy of Errors*, and *One Flew Over the Cuckoo's Nest*.

Jackie came to see John in some of the shows, and while she was glad that her son enjoyed the stage, she was not keen on acting as a possible career choice for him. Jackie was more interested in seeing John do well in his other subjects and had become concerned after a teacher indicated that John had the potential to do better in school. Things grew especially tense when John failed the exam at Phillips that students are required to take at the end of eleventh grade. The test covered five subjects, including math, which had never been John's strong suit. As a result of his low score John had to repeat the eleventh grade. The test results upset Jackie, but she was grateful that the school had agreed to give her son a second chance, as students who fail the exam are usually asked to leave.

Although she was in New York while John was at school, Jackie believed that her son still needed her guidance. Therefore, while many of John's school pals spent their summers pursuing recreational activities in Europe and elsewhere, Jackie planned some character-building

*J*ohn tried to be an average teenage kid who did average teenage things.
But photographers invariably found him, whether he was on a motorcycle in
New Jersey or on a boat in Maine. And he was always a Kennedy, with all
the obligations that came with being a member of America's first family.

*I*n 1979,
Caroline, John,
and Jackie
attended the dedi-
cation ceremony
for the JFK
Library in Boston.

experiences for her teenage son. In June 1977, John enrolled in a wilderness survival course with the Outward Bound program. Besides receiving instruction in sailing, rock climbing, and first aid, participants were left out in the wilderness for three days with just a gallon of water, some pots, several matches, and a text on edible plants. Success on these outings supposedly instilled a renewed sense of confidence and strength in participants, and that's what John's mother wanted for him.

During the summer of 1978, Jackie arranged for John to spend six weeks working in Wyoming as a wrangler at the Bar Cross Ranch. She was assured by the owner, John Perry Barlow, that her son would be treated like any other ranch hand rather than as America's crown prince. Knowing that toughness was an inherent part of success, Jackie felt that John needed some contrast to the cushioned existence he was accustomed to. "His mother sent him out West," Barlow said in describing how JFK Jr.'s stint at his ranch came about. "She rather unceremoniously kicked him out of the nest and dumped him into the lap of a Republican rancher from Wyoming."[11]

John rose to the challenge as he put his all into the backbreaking work of driving cattle, repairing barbed-wire fences, and building dams. The ranch hands who had all expected a pampered rich kid were amazed at the energy and effort that John brought to the job, and everyone around him enjoyed his warmth and sense of humor. John Perry Barlow claimed that while his relationship with John started out as that of a father and son, it grew and changed over time until the two were more like brothers.

After John graduated from Phillips Academy, he surprised many people with the college he chose to attend. The Kennedys were a Harvard family—John's grandfather, father, and three uncles went there. His sister, Caroline, had chosen it as well and was now a student there. John, however, selected a different path and enrolled at Brown University in Providence, Rhode Island, where a more relaxed, free-spirited atmosphere seemed to prevail. Brown was also the Ivy League university that appeared to be drawing the offspring of prominent Democratic families. President Jimmy Carter's daughter, Amy, went there, as did Walter Mondale's son, Billy. Mondale was Carter's vice president as well as the Democratic nominee for president in 1984.

At Brown, as always, John made friends easily and got along well. He and another student named Randall Poster organized a student discussion group, which delved into pressing contemporary issues such as conditions in South Africa, arms control, and civil rights. "John had definite opinions on things, but he also argued on both sides of the issue," a friend recalled. "He was definitely passionate about civil rights for everyone in our society."[12] After visiting South Africa one summer while at Brown, John was appalled by the horrors of apartheid—the nation's system of segregation, which sharply curtailed the rights of non-whites. Determined to alert his fellow students to this injustice, he arranged for former United Nations ambassador Andrew Young to give a lecture at the university on that topic.

Although John shunned his celebrity status, he nevertheless possessed a tremendous amount of personal magnetism that set him apart from the crowd. "People gravitated towards him," explained John's fraternity brother Richard Wiese in describing the phenomenon. "He was used to a lot of women who would melt in front of him."[13] John's fraternity, Phi Kappa Psi, took full advantage of John's legendary ability to attract females without trying. Once, his fraternity brothers put out a sign that JFK Jr. would be at the house for a party, and young women wanting to attend stood in line for blocks.

The ongoing female presence in John's life, however, remained his mother and sister, to whom he was extremely close despite the miles separating them. Jackie visited John at Brown when she could, although she was sometimes surprised by what she found. Living in his fraternity house, John had developed poor housekeeping habits, and he and his roommate were known to have one of the messiest rooms. Once while his mother was visiting, she needed to use the phone in John's room, and he wasn't around at the moment. Richard Wiese took her up to her son's room, but that apparently was easier to find than the phone. Wiese said:

> [Looking for the phone, Jackie] was down on the floor on her hands and knees following the wires through the clothes. It turned out to be a wire from the stereo. She ended up using the phone in my room, and she told him [John] that my room was neater and that he should be more like me.[14]

While at Brown, John was also known to be absentminded. "He lost more bikes and stuff than anybody," Richard Wiese continued, "and used to walk around with his keys attached to his pants, like a custodian, because he'd lose them all the time."[15] This casual attitude sometimes extended to clothing items that Kennedy borrowed from friends. Once Wiese lent John a blazer for a special occasion, with disastrous results. "Somebody hit him with a meatball during dinner," Wiese related. John told his fraternity brother, "I'll take it to the laundry." "Three weeks later," Wiese added, "I saw it behind the couch, all rolled up in a ball. But you couldn't get mad at him. You cut him more slack than you did most people."[16]

One reason those around him were so understanding was that Kennedy was such a wonderful friend. CNN

Chief International Correspondent Christine Amanpour met John when he was a student at Brown. They shared a house together along with some other students. Like so many of his relationships, their friendship stood the test of time. Amanpour would say a number of years later:

> We were friends almost from the beginning. But the thing about John is that his friendships speak to the man himself. He is a man who has kept the friends that he has made throughout life. He is a loyal and generous and faithful guy, and if you look at his friends, they are all the people who have been with him for the last nearly forty years of his life. And I think that is very, very, very important to realize that about this man. He wasn't swept away by the life he led, by the riches he had, by the fame.[17]

Though everyone always seemed to want to be around John, the personal radar he developed helped him to separate the social climbers from those who just liked him for himself. Some saw John as a natural people-magnet, who might have been student body president if he hadn't wanted to stay out of the limelight because of his name.

At Brown, John's acting talent once again emerged. He had roles in such college productions as *The Tempest*, *The Playboy of the Western World*, *Volpone*, *Short Eyes*, and *In the Boom Boom Room*. Often, leaving his fraternity house for these productions in full costume made John a ripe target for practical jokes. In one such instance, when some friends dropped water balloons on him, John remained a good sport. "He took it all in real good stride," recalled Rick Guy, a fraternity brother. "He just ran back upstairs and cleaned himself up. It's not as if he started yelling or swearing at anyone. He was obviously perturbed, but he didn't verbalize it. He was a classy guy."[18] Another friend agreed: "I've never seen him intentionally lash out with malice or deliberately do anything to hurt somebody. He hasn't got a vengeful bone in his body."[19]

John worked hard on his stage roles and was reportedly quite good. Many thought that his good looks and demeanor on stage made him perfect for the theater. Another of the student actors at Brown marveled at Kennedy's seemingly inborn acting ability and said that "without ever having set foot in the Actors Studio, [John was] echoing the approach of Brando and Nicholson among others."[20] But John's acting ability wasn't appreciated by just his fellow actors. As Don Wilmeth, professor of theater, speech, and dance at Brown, said of John, "He's a very sound actor, very directable. If he had taken theater seriously, he could have been wonderful."[21]

Had Kennedy ever planed on a career in acting? Friends say that though he was an American history major, he had considered attending Yale University School of Drama after graduation. Biographers as well as those close to Kennedy claim that his mother was firmly against it and that he reluctantly bowed to her wishes. "His mother laid down the law," a classmate at Brown noted. "She told John in no uncertain terms that acting was beneath him, that he was his father's son, and that he had a tradition of public service to uphold." The student went on to say that John and his mother "really had terrible fights over this." "John is pretty good at controlling his temper," he added, "but there were times when he talked about his mother when he just lost it. What he wanted from her was respect, and for a while there he just didn't feel as if he had it."[22]

While John was still at Brown, Robert Stigwood, who had produced the movie *Saturday Night Fever*, offered him the chance to play the part of his father in a film based on President Kennedy's early life. John wanted the part, but his mother insisted that he finish college. When John asked if after college he could do anything he wanted, Jackie reportedly told him, "Anything but act."

"Jackie made it clear that John was the standard bearer of Camelot. She didn't want him to act," noted Christopher Andersen, who has written extensively on the Kennedys.[23] She felt that John needed to choose a worthwhile career, but there was another reason as well. Jackie had always feared that attempts might be made on her children's lives, and she knew acting would place John more prominently on display.

The former First Lady had long been the major parental figure in John's life, and while she was soft-spoken, Jacqueline Kennedy Onassis could be extremely persuasive. "When you got anywhere near Jackie," commented her half-brother James Auchincloss, "you didn't think about anything but Jackie. She sucked all the oxygen out of the air for 100 miles around.... You didn't get into any arguments with her and you never said 'no.' Nobody did."[24] Years later when interviewed, John would deny that his mother dissuaded him from acting, claiming that it had never been more than a hobby. However, there are those who find his denial difficult to believe.

In any case, by his junior year at Brown, John had noticeably changed. He moved off campus and shared a house with several other students. He kept his room clean and his car immaculate. "John was no longer a booze-guzzling rebellious slob," a friend said in commenting on the metamorphosis.[25] John also had a new girlfriend named Sally Munro, who was a student at Brown as well. She looked so much like John's sister that Sally was frequently mistaken for Caroline. Jackie liked Sally—John had picked an intelligent young woman from a good family who seemed to bring out the best in her son.

John broke with family tradition by attending Brown instead of Harvard, where his father, uncles, and sister had gone. Nor had any other Kennedy shown an interest in acting, as John did throughout prep school and college. During his freshman year he played the role of Bonario in Ben Jonson's *Volpone*. But by the time Jackie, Caroline, and Uncle Teddy attended his graduation in 1983, there was one thing certain about his future choice of careers: John F. Kennedy Jr. was not going to become an actor.

During the summer of his junior year at Brown, John spent six weeks tutoring low-income teens in a program sponsored by the University of Connecticut. In many ways John was changing and maturing, and those who knew and loved him saw the promise of wonderful things to come. The public was still intent on following the future of the prince of Camelot as well. Reporters throughout the United States and from a number of foreign countries covered his graduation from Brown University on June 6, 1983.

Chapter 5

A Young Man in Demand

N ow a college graduate, John took some time off to go to India. His mother had always loved that country, which was one of the few places where the Kennedys seemed able to escape the continual glare of photographers' flashbulbs. John's grandmother, Rose Kennedy, had often quoted the biblical saying: "To whom much has been given much will be required." Tutoring children in the slums of Delhi and studying vital public-health issues there, John carried on the Kennedy tradition of charitable work. Understanding that this was an important time for him, Sally Munro joined John during his stay in the foreign land.

Back in the United States, however, things had not gone as smoothly for other members of the Kennedy clan. Several of John's cousins experienced drug-related problems. Bobby Jr. was arrested for heroin possession in the summer of 1983, and just a year later his brother David was found dead in a motel room of a drug overdose. It was a tragic end to an ongoing battle with addiction the young man had waged. Other Kennedy cousins Patrick Kennedy and Chris Lawford would struggle with drug dependency as well, but they were able to overcome the problem.

To Jackie's relief John continued on a straighter path, and after returning from India spent the next few years working for nonprofit agencies as well as traveling. While he still dated Sally Munro, they were neither married nor engaged, and many women saw the handsome, dashing, wealthy heir to Camelot as fair game. This included the sultry singer-actress Madonna, who had left John a number of telephone messages suggesting that they meet. She and John had a few dates—it was the first time John dated someone who was more famous and in demand than he. His mother didn't care for this departure in taste from the classy Sally Munro and had called John several times to see if there was anything to the relationship. There wasn't, and Jackie was relieved as John and Madonna decided to remain just friends.

Madonna might have been the first Hollywood type that John dated, but she wouldn't be the last. Besides liking actresses, John was also still drawn to the stage. While in New York in August 1985 he took a role in an off-Broadway production entitled *Winners* at the Irish Arts Center. Once again those around him saw potential in Kennedy as a budding talent. Nye Heron, the executive director of the Irish Arts Center, cited John as "one of the best young actors I've seen in years."[1] The play was a tremendous success and there were several offers to produce it on Broadway with the original cast. When asked about a future on the stage, however, John told the press: "This is definitely not a professional acting debut by any means. It's just a hobby."[2]

John had recently begun dating Christina Haag, his costar in the play, whom he met at Brown and who was now a drama student at Juilliard. Jackie was far more approving of Christina than of Madonna, but after a time that relationship ended as well. John would date many women, as the number of women wanting to meet him seemed endless. In 1986 he was selected one of the most eligible bachelors in America by the 10,000 members of the organization Manwatchers. Shortly afterward, *People Weekly* magazine named him "America's Most Eligible Bachelor." Later on, in 1988, the magazine would proclaim John "The Sexiest Man Alive." Such titles only compounded what John had to deal with when it came to women. In those days it was even difficult for him to go out on his own without being approached by females he didn't know. Bryan Reidy, the manager at Gallagher's Steak House in Manhattan, observed how "women would brush into him [Kennedy] at the bar so they could say, 'I touched John!' "[3]

*A*merica's most eligible bachelor would remain single for some years yet, but his sister Caroline had found her true love. Caroline was going to marry Edwin Schlossberg, and John would be the best man at the wedding. Caroline had been an important influence in his life. As a college buddy of John's explained it, "He and Caroline were best friends. There was genuine love between them."[4] John himself acknowledged the family's closeness when he accepted his brother-in-law's place in the family with a wedding toast that began: "All our lives there's just been the three of us: Mommy, Caroline and me."[5]

If Ed Schlossberg was Caroline's dream, then Jackie's dream also came true in September 1986, when to her delight John started law school at New York University. "Now I can die a happy woman," Jackie had jokingly said after John decided to attend.[6] As always, it didn't take John

John and his cousin Maria Shriver at Caroline's wedding in 1986. Jackie had managed to keep that event from becoming a media circus. But there was nothing she could do two years later, when People splashed John's picture on its cover—ratcheting up attention by the public and press to almost fanatical levels. John took the hoopla in good grace, even joking there were much worse things to be than "The Sexiest Man Alive."

Kate Hepburn: Memories of a maverick girlhood

People weekly

John F. Kennedy Jr.

THE SEXIEST MAN ALIVE (1988)

long to make friends and fit in with the rest of the student body. An embarrassing issue, however, came up while he was at NYU. John's housekeeping skills had slipped again, and when he moved out of the apartment he had sublet on West 86 Street, his landlord charged that the dwelling had been left in "an obnoxious condition." To correct the damage, the floors would need resanding, a new carpet would have to be installed, some holes in the walls would need patching. The landlord sued John to collect the money for repairs. Fortunately for John, the case was settled out of court.

John's years in law school were largely uneventful, and to some degree the press backed off a bit. Nevertheless, John took center stage at the 1988 National Democratic Convention in Atlanta, Georgia, when he introduced his uncle Ted Kennedy with a brief speech. John began:

> Over a quarter of a century ago, my father stood before you to accept the nomination for the presidency of the United States. So many of you came into public service because of him. In a very real sense, because of you, he is with us still. And for that I am grateful to all of you."[7]

When he finished, the audience gave the slain president's son a two-minute standing ovation. Nearly everyone was impressed by his poise, charm, and sincerity. It was instantly clear to many of the movers and shakers in the Democratic party that JFK's son had enormous political potential. "It was fantastic," former White House press secretary Pierre Salinger commented after seeing John in action. "I was telling him that this speech showed strongly that John Jr. should start thinking about going into politics. He said he was interested but he was still too young. He told me that he had an idea that he should go into politics in the next century."[8] Sadly, just eleven years later, the world would learn that John F. Kennedy Jr. would not live to see the next century.

At that time, however, John's future looked brighter than ever. He graduated from law school in May 1989 and went to work as an assistant district attorney in Manhattan, where he was assigned to the special prosecution bureau. People who worked with him were amazed by what an "everyday guy" this wealthy celebrity was. He never arrived at work in a limo—instead he would ride his bike or take the subway. Normally, the press would not be interested in the work of a fledgling assistant DA, but because of who he was everything he did was scrutinized. For the most part his positive strides went unreported, but any blunder that could sell newspapers or magazines made headlines. Trying his first case, John fumbled a bit on what was thought to be a shoo-in conviction. It involved a burglary in which the accused was apprehended on the premises. John won the case, but his minor errors were nevertheless considered newsworthy. Sometimes it seemed as if the media were determined to stake out John's office. Reporters tailed him to restaurants when he went out to lunch and reported what he ate. A paralegal at the office who made about $15,000 a year was offered $10,000 to take a picture of John on his first day on the job.

To John's embarrassment, he failed the difficult 12-hour New York State bar examination in July 1989 and took it a second time in February 1990. This time he was just eleven points short of passing, but the media were merciless and *The New York Post* ran a banner headline proclaiming: "THE HUNK FLUNKS." In commenting on Kennedy's performance, his college chum Peter Burrow said:

A star is born. When John F. Kennedy Jr. addressed
the Democratic National Convention in 1988, party leaders
began to envision a second coming of Camelot.

John is very bright but he had so much attention and has always avoided getting boxed in. I think on the bar exam he did get boxed in. The whole world was watching and the pressure mounted, so he started playing against himself. But that wasn't a reflection on his intelligence.[9]

John dealt with the negative publicity as gracefully as he could under the circumstances. Acknowledging to the press that he was disappointed with the test results as well as publicly admitting that he was "not a major legal genius," the young attorney added, "But, you know, God willing, I'll be back there in July and I'll pass it then or I'll pass it when I'm 95."[10] Kennedy didn't have to wait nearly that long. He passed it on the third try.

During this period in John Jr.'s life he did more than just work as an assistant DA and study for the bar exam. He also became involved in a number of important projects. He helped design Mental Retardation and Developmental Disabilities Studies, a program funded by the Joseph P. Kennedy Jr. Foundation, which provides funding to train students to work with the disabled. In 1989, John founded Reaching Up, a nonprofit organization to assist those working with the mentally challenged. He also became involved with the Robin Hood Foundation, which provides afterschool care, food programs, and job training to those in need. John was a member of President Clinton's Committee on Mental Retardation and served on the board of the Institute of Politics at the John F. Kennedy School of Government at Harvard.

John was also vice-chairman of the John F. Kennedy Library Foundation established in 1984 to support the Kennedy Library in preserving and exhibiting the essence of President Kennedy's life. In addition, John and his sister,

Jackie and Caroline beam with pride at John's graduation from New York University Law School in May 1989. Three months later he started work as an assistant district attorney in Manhattan. On his first day at the job, John was besieged by reporters and even neighborhood policemen asked for his autograph. But the famous young man proved to be a pleasant surprise to his coworkers. He rode his bike to the office, never asked for or expected special treatment, and won convictions in every case he argued. Still, it wasn't the career for him. John confessed that he sympathized with the defendants he was supposed to prosecute. "My instinct was to help them, not punish them," he said.

In 1989, John and Jackie—seated under a portrait of President Kennedy—visited the JFK Library to publicize the creation of the Profile in Courage Award. After John's death, the library announced that donations made in his name would be used to endow the award, which had meant so much to him throughout the last decade of his life.

Caroline, organized the Profile in Courage Award in 1989, which was inspired by their father's Pulitzer Prize-winning book *Profiles in Courage*. The text is an account of eight men in American politics whose principles and integrity made them models of courage. To honor the slain president, the award is given to individuals in politics who exemplify the high standards that Kennedy wrote about. It is presented each year on or near May 29—JFK's birthday.

John Kennedy Jr. was also active socially and, as usual, did not lack female companionship. Admitting a weakness for beautiful women, he had a number of dates with such dazzling models as Cindy Crawford and Julie Baker. John also dated Hollywood actresses Sarah Jessica Parker and, more significantly, Daryl Hannah. Hannah and John seemed quite smitten with one another and had a lot in common. They seemed genuinely compatible emotionally, and both were extremely athletic and loved outdoor sports. Those who were close to the couple felt that the actress sincerely cared for John and wanted only the best for him. People joked that the two had similar lifestyles—they were rich people who enjoyed playing at being poor.

Their five-year relationship sometimes faltered, however. One reason had to do with Daryl's feelings for Jackson Browne, a singer with whom she had lived for a time. Daryl would get close to John, only to be drawn back to Jackson and then try to work things out with the singer. After a serious confrontation with Browne, she called John. Always protective of women, John acted like a true knight and came to her rescue. The two grew especially close after that. They began living together in Daryl's New York City apartment, and after the actress was spotted buying a wedding dress at a flea market, there were rumors of an upcoming wedding.

They never married, though Daryl Hannah was at John's side when he learned that his mother was suffering from a form of cancer called non-Hodgkin's lymphoma. During this period, John gave a great deal of support to his mother, who had always been available for him. John and Jackie took many long walks together in Central Park during the winter and spring of 1994. After Jackie lost her battle with the disease that May, John announced her death to the world. Standing in front of the Fifth Avenue apartment building where he had grown up and his mother still lived, John somberly told reporters:

> Last night, at around 10:15, my mother passed on. She was surrounded by her friends and family and her books and the people and things that she loved. And she did it in her own way, and we all feel lucky for that, and now she's in God's hands.[11]

President Clinton acknowledged the nation's loss with the death of this elegant former First Lady. He comforted John and Caroline and publicly said of their mother:

> God gave her very great gifts, and imposed on her great burdens. She bore them all with dignity, grace, and uncommon common sense. In the end, she cared most about being a good mother to her children, and the lives of Caroline and John leave no doubt that she was that and more.[12]

Thousands of people across the country were saddened as they realized that another remembrance of Camelot was gone. Now more than ever, people looked to John to carry forth the Kennedy banner. Would he go into politics? It was an unanswered question at that time and, unfortunately, would remain so.

It seemed that the entire nation grieved along with John and Caroline, shown here outside the church after their mother's funeral in May 1994. When John's plane went down on a Friday night in July little more than five years later, a Time journalist wrote, "In the pain of last Saturday, it was possible to be grateful that Jackie had died first, this woman who had taught the country how to mourn in grace. We could not have borne to watch her bury her son."

Almost everyone expected that John F. Kennedy Jr.
would run for office. Instead, he chose to combine his parents'
occupations—politics and publishing—in a magazine that covered politicians as celebrities. By founding **George**, John at last
became the man he wanted to be, instead of the man both history
and the Kennedy name had seemingly required him to be. Yet
despite his burdensome legacy, John was just a regular guy at
work. He brought his dog to the office, bought pizzas for the staff,
and gave his employees tickets to a World Series game. John even
rode the subway with them uptown to Yankee Stadium.

Chapter *6*

His Own Person

*I*n some ways, John truly came into his own following his mother's death. Having left his job as assistant district attorney in 1993, John was now ready to take on an exciting business venture. In 1995, he launched a new magazine called *George* (named after the country's first president), which has been characterized as a mixture of politics and celebrity.

Ironically, the man who had dodged the media all his life now became part of it. His glossy monthly publication glowed with pictures of chic political fund-raisers and potential makeovers of dowdy politicians. When the magazine's first issue was criticized for having on its cover a bare-midriffed Cindy Crawford in a powdered wig and ruffled shirt posing as George Washington, Kennedy defended his choice, saying that "political magazines should look like *Mirabella*."[1] Yet despite all the fluff there was also some serious journalism.

In an Editor's Letter he wrote for an issue of *George,* John explained the magazine's purpose:

Why create a magazine about politics? We believe that if we can make politics accessible by covering it in an entertaining and compelling way, popular interest and involvement will follow. But calling *George* a political magazine isn't entirely accurate, since we aim to be a breed apart from traditional political magazines. Recognizing that interest in "inside Washington" is thin beyond the Beltway, we will define politics extravagantly, from elected officials to media moguls to movie stars to ordinary citizens. And we will cover it exuberantly, showing the unexpected, meaningful, and whimsical ways it affects your daily life.[2]

Kennedy knew that his name and allure were the driving force behind the magazine, and he more readily made public appearances and gave interviews to promote it. By keeping a high profile, Kennedy managed to draw celebrities for his covers, but he also became involved in the essence of the publication. He was a hands-on editor, regularly assigning stories and editing manuscripts. Journalist Steven Brill noted:

[John] is someone who despite the fame he had and despite all the advantages he had, was willing to undertake something that was very difficult because he believed in it, and he came to work early in the morning and left late, and he was hard at work in the process of evolving a very interesting and very original magazine. And I think he deserves an enormous amount of credit for that. It was not something he had to do, but he did it.[3]

Kennedy also did some interesting interviews with a wide range of people you might not expect to find in a magazine

The observed had become the observer. *Few people turned down John's request to interview them for George. His eclectic choices of people to feature in the magazine included even his father's archenemy, Fidel Castro. Here John is shown in 1997 with another of his subjects, the Dalai Lama.*

like George. These included Louis Farrakhan, Billy Graham, and Garth Brooks.

There were other important changes in John's life. He and Daryl Hannah broke up for good in 1994, and about that time he found the person he would call his true soulmate. A strikingly attractive young woman named Carolyn Bessette proved to be the perfect princess for Camelot. Nearly 6 feet (183 cm) tall, the willowy blonde was the epitome of style and grace. In the words of John's uncle Ted she was "the new pride of the Kennedys." In many ways Carolyn was an ideal choice for John. She was Catholic, and while she did not physically resemble Jackie, Carolyn had the same air of elegance and softspokenness about her. Some pointed out that both women even had lilting French maiden names, Bouvier and Bessette.

Carolyn had been raised in the affluent suburban town of Greenwich, Connecticut, by her mother Ann, a school administrator, and her stepfather, Richard Freeman, a successful orthopedic surgeon. Carolyn had stood out in the crowd even in her youth. At St. Mary's High School she was voted the Ultimate Beautiful Person by her classmates. As one of them, Claudia Slocum, put it, "Carolyn was the only girl who could pull off wearing the ill-fitting school uniform pants."[4]

Bessette earned a degree in education from Boston University, where she posed for the cover of a "B.U.'s Most Beautiful Women" calendar. Carolyn considered a modeling career but decided that it wasn't right for her. "She couldn't sit still long enough," a photographer later told a New York newspaper. "I think she's so smart, she wanted a better job."[5] Bessette passed on a career in education as well and was quoted in 1992 as saying: "At the time I felt a little underdeveloped myself to be completely responsible for twenty-five other people's children. And to a large extent, I felt it wouldn't be provocative enough for me."[6]

The fashion industry seemed the perfect place for a woman with trendsetting style, and Carolyn quickly rose up through the ranks of Calvin Klein's fashion empire. Starting off in Boston, within a year she was promoted and brought to the company's New York headquarters where she earned an impressive salary as a publicist as well as a personal shopper for many of the designer's celebrity clients. Carolyn traveled in New York's best social circles and was accustomed to dating handsome successful men whom most other women only dreamed about.

*T*here are different stories about how Carolyn and John met. Some people say she caught his eye while both were jogging in Central Park. Others claim that they were introduced by Calvin Klein's wife, Kelly, at a charity benefit. Regardless of the circumstances, few would deny that there was a strong mutual attraction between Bessette and Kennedy. "They had instant eye lock," Paul Wilmot, a publicist and Carolyn's former boss said. "The minute they saw each other they were mad for one another. He called her the next day."[7]

Their subsequent romance was chronicled by photographers nearly everywhere the couple went. They were often seen hugging, kissing, and walking hand in hand. Details of a stormy lover's quarrel they had in a park in February 1996 found their way into the tabloids. During the spat, Kennedy had snatched the engagement ring off Carolyn's finger, only to sit down on a curb afterward and cry. Carolyn came over to him, and the couple made up moments later. She obviously meant far more to John than other women had. John's old fraternity brother Richard Wiese commented in describing John's enchantment with the new woman in his life: "A lot of girls put on airs around him and that really turned him off. Carolyn was very provocative. She challenged him and made him think."[8]

Carolyn began living with John in his loft in the chic downtown Manhattan neighborhood of Tribeca. The couple enjoyed their surroundings, frequently going to local restaurants and diners and taking long walks with their dog, Friday. Friends said that John liked watching Carolyn navigate difficult social situations with her characteristic charm. "She had a supernatural empathy about her, a truly sincere way of dealing with people," remarked Kennedy's longtime friend John Perry Barlow.[9] She was also wonderful with John's nieces and nephew, Caroline's children. They loved watching her do somersaults as she cheered for her husband's team in family touch-football games.

Thousands of women would have done just about anything to marry John F. Kennedy Jr., but Carolyn took her time before saying yes. "She was excited," Bessette's college friend Dana Gallo Strayton said, "but she wanted to be sure it was the right decision."[10] Once she accepted, the couple planned a top-secret wedding on Cumberland Island off the coast of Georgia. The ceremony, attended by only forty family members and close friends, took place on September 21, 1996, in a tiny wood-frame chapel that was formerly a slave church. It had no electricity; the only light came from candles and kerosene lamps. At least one guest remarked that the wedding had an almost fairytale quality to it. The bride looked magnificent in a $40,000 floor-length white silk crepe gown that had been designed for the occasion. She wore no jewelry and carried a small bouquet of lilies of the valley. Their wedding proved to be a rare and cherished private moment for the couple. John did such a fine job of keeping things from the press that some joked he should be in the Secret Service.

His mother had spent much of her life trying to elude the media, but John managed to outdo even Jackie in keeping under wraps his intimate and hush-hush wedding ceremony with Carolyn Bessette.

In March 1998, President Clinton took the Kennedys on a tour of John's first home. Their visit included a look at JFK's official portrait, which hangs in the mansion.

John and Carolyn Kennedy lived in the spotlight, while struggling to maintain a normal lifestyle. Wherever they went, the two were robbed of privacy by the stares of strangers and the intrusive flash of cameras. Yet after the plane crash in which they died, a friend observed that the Kennedys had been "a very warm, happy couple"— who laughed a lot together.

In some ways Carolyn and John had a very traditional marriage. Carolyn had quit her job a few months prior to the wedding. She took cooking lessons, spent time with her friends, and offered advice on various aspects of her husband's magazine. "She was very much Mrs. John Kennedy in an old-fashioned way," a friend said. "He [John] didn't want a wife that went to the office. He liked the fact that she was there when he came home."[11] They even had pet names for one another—he called her "Kitty Cat" and she called him "Mouse."

The press hungrily watched the newlyweds. John, who had grown up dodging photographers, was accustomed to media attention and at times even used it to promote his magazine, *George*. With Carolyn it was another story. "Nothing prepared her for the impact of all the attention," noted Richard Holbrooke, United Nations ambassador-designate. "It was very troubling to her that she couldn't get out of the house. She was besieged."[12] John tried to convince the press to give his wife some breathing room, but he met with limited success. Like his mother, more than anything Carolyn craved privacy.

There was speculation that living in a fish bowl had taken its toll on the marriage. More than one gossip columnist noted that Carolyn often looked upset. But those closest to the couple told a different story. At their wedding rehearsal dinner, John had toasted his bride-to-be and declared, "I am the happiest man alive." Their friends and family members claim that the pair's feelings for one another only deepened with time. Reportedly, Carolyn and John hoped to have children before long—John said he especially wanted a son they would name Flynn. Though they loved New York, the couple now spoke about finding a place outside the city to raise their family, and they were excited about the prospects ahead. As Paul Wilmot summed it up, "The next five years should have been great for them."[13]

Chapter 7

Gone Too Soon

John F. Kennedy Jr. knew that his family was sometimes viewed as America's royalty, and in an interview he once admitted, "I understand that my father is part of the mythology of this country."[1] Young Kennedy, however, didn't see himself as the heir apparent, and in 1993 said: "It's hard for me to talk about a legacy or a mystique. It's my family. It's my mother. It's my sister. It's my father. We're a family like any other. We look out for one another. The fact that there have been difficulties and hardships makes us closer."[2]

Nevertheless, America felt that the Kennedys were part of its family, too, and as they seemed to endure more than their share of tragedy, the myth of the Kennedy curse arose. In the 1940s, President Kennedy's older brother Joseph P. Kennedy Jr. was killed in a dangerous World War II air mission. The President's sister Kathleen died in a private plane crash in 1948. During the 1960s both JFK and his brother Bobby were assassinated. Later, two of Bobby's sons would die young: David of a drug overdose, and his brother Michael in a skiing accident. John Jr.'s infant brother, Patrick, died just days after his birth and, finally, there was the loss of John and his wife, Carolyn, in a plane crash.

John F. Kennedy Jr., however, saw himself as blessed rather than cursed, and often joked about the so-called "curse." If he fumbled while playing football, for example, he might say something like, "Ah, the Kennedy curse."

There are those who argue that it's wrong to look at the Kennedy family tragedies without examining the element of risk involved in the various incidents. Kennedy men were generally taught early on that to live cautiously was to live on the sidelines. "Men are not made for safe havens," his uncle Bobby told John, and that creed was embodied in the behavior and choices of many of the family members.[3]

Joe Kennedy Jr. died after volunteering for what some believe was a suicide mission, and his sister Kathleen took that flight to meet with her father despite poor weather conditions. The meeting had been important to both Kathleen and her divorced Protestant boyfriend who accompanied her. They were hoping to convince Kathleen's father to agree to their marriage.

Recklessness was a factor in Michael Kennedy's death—he skied into a tree while tossing a football. Although John's accident cannot be compared to that of his cousin Michael, a trustee of the Kennedy family trust, John Whitehead, noted that John "had a certain daredevil quality to him...." He added, "[John] had a sense that 'there is nothing I can't cope with myself.'"[4]

In the final analysis, John F. Kennedy Jr. lived his life in his own way. He had come to terms with his family name and celebrity and was carving out a unique path for himself. His life was a work in progress, and he had begun to toy with the idea of going into politics in the future. John had been frequently asked by New York Democrats to run for office. Some say he had considered running for the U.S. Senate in 2000 if Hillary Clinton didn't.

We will never know what JFK Jr. might have become, but we do know what he was. As his uncle Senator Edward M. Kennedy said in his nephew's eulogy:

> ...John was so much more than those long-ago images emblazoned in our minds. He was a boy who grew into a man with a zest for life and a love of adventure. He was a Pied Piper who brought us all along....John's father taught us...to reach for the moon and the stars. John did that in all he did....[He] was a serious man who brightened our lives with his smile and his grace. He was a son of privilege who founded a program called Reaching Up to train better caregivers for the mentally disabled. He joined Wall Street executives on the Robin Hood Foundation to help the city's impoverished children. And he did it all so quietly, without ever calling attention to himself.
>
> John was one of Jackie's two miracles. He was still becoming the person he would be, and doing it by the beat of his own drummer. He had only just begun. There was in him a great promise of things to come.
>
> We dared to think that this John Kennedy would live to comb gray hair....But like his father he had every gift but length of years. We who have loved him from the day he was born, and watched the remarkable man he became, now bid him farewell.[5]

A card placed outside John's apartment after word of his death reached the public may have expressed how many Americans felt. It contained just one line from Shakespeare. The note read: "Good Night, Sweet Prince." Those who imagined John F. Kennedy Jr. in America's broader future are left to dream of what might have been.

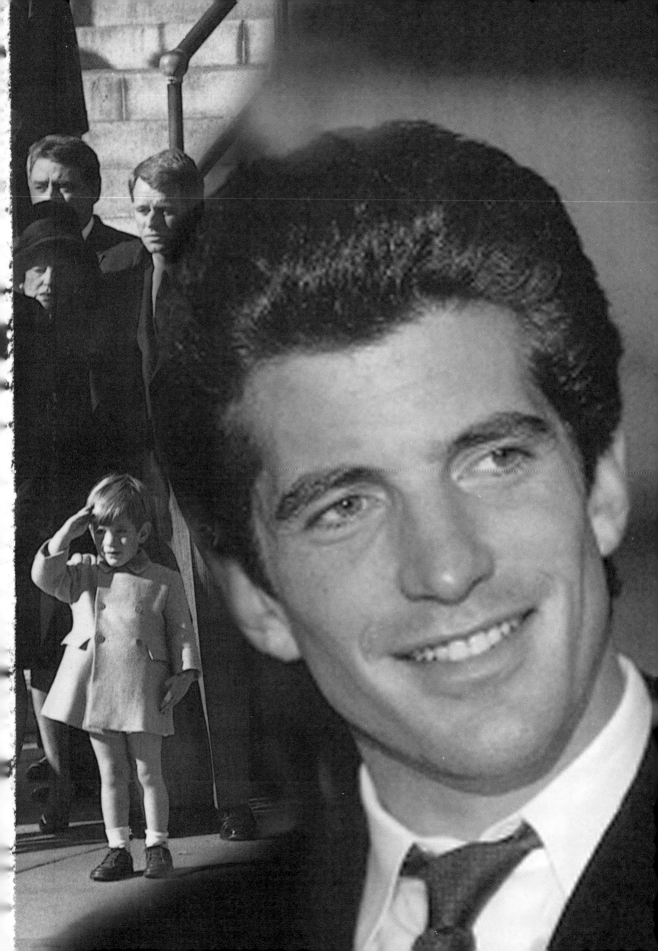

John F. Kennedy Jr.
Timeline

1960	John F. Kennedy Jr. is born on November 25, becoming the first child ever born to a president-elect. He weighed 6 pounds 3 ounces (3 kg).
1963	Patrick Bouvier Kennedy, John Jr.'s infant brother, dies on August 9 of a lung ailment just days after his birth.
1963	President John F. Kennedy is assassinated while riding in a motorcade in Dallas. The assassination takes place on November 22, only three days before John's third birthday.
1964	Jacqueline Kennedy and her children move to New York City. They live in an apartment building on Fifth Avenue, and John often plays in Central Park.
1965	John starts school at St. David's in New York City, where his cousin William Kennedy Smith is also enrolled.

1968	John's uncle Bobby Kennedy is assassinated on June 6.
1968	Jacqueline Kennedy marries billionaire shipping tycoon Aristotle Onassis. John and his sister, Caroline, now have a stepfather.
1971	In December, John appears in a Collegiate school production of the musical *Oliver!*
1973	On January 22, Aristotle Onassis's only son, Alexander, is killed in a plane crash. He and John had grown extremely close.
1974	After slipping away from his Secret Service bodyguards, John is mugged in Central Park. His ten-speed Italian-made bicycle is taken.
1975	Aristotle Onassis dies of bronchial pneumonia on March 15.
1976	John enters Phillips Academy, a prestigious prep school in Andover, Massachusetts.
1976	In June, John and his cousin Timothy Shriver work as volunteers in an earthquake relief program in Guatemala.
1977	John participates in an Outward Bound wilderness survival course that summer.
1978	During the summer John spends six weeks working as a wrangler at the Bar Cross Ranch in Wyoming.
1979	In September, John enrolls as a freshman at Brown University.
1980	In March, John plays Bonario, a professional soldier in the play *Volpone*. It was the first play he appeared in at Brown. There would be others.
1982	During the summer, John and his cousin Timothy Shriver tutor teens from low-income families through a program at the University of Connecticut.

1983	John graduates from Brown University on June 6. He majored in American History.
1983	John leaves for India in October. While there, he tutors children and studies public-health issues.
1985	John takes the male lead in the play *Winners* at the Irish Arts Center in New York City.
1986	The members of the organization Manwatchers vote John one of the most eligible bachelors in America. The same year *People Weekly* magazine names him "America's Most Eligible Bachelor." That June, his sister, Caroline, marries Ed Schlossberg. John is best man at their wedding.
1986	John enrolls in New York University's law school.
1988	John introduces his uncle Ted Kennedy at the National Democratic Convention with a moving speech reminiscent of his father. He receives a standing ovation and is recognized as having tremendous political potential. *People Weekly* magazine proclaims John the "Sexiest Man Alive."
1989	John graduates from law school and takes a job as an assistant district attorney in Manhattan. John helps develop the Mental Retardation and Developmental Disabilities Program. Kennedy starts Reaching Up, a nonprofit group to benefit those working with the mentally disabled.
1990	John passes the New York State bar examination on his third try.
1993	Kennedy resigns from his job at the DA's office with a perfect conviction record.
1994	Jacqueline Kennedy Onassis, John's mother, dies of non-Hodgkin's lymphoma.
1995 —	Kennedy officially launches his magazine

George on September 8 at a news conference in Manhattan. He jokingly tells reporters that he hadn't seen so many of them in one place since he failed his first bar exam.

1996   John and Carolyn Bessette marry on September 21 in a small private ceremony on Cumberland Island off the coast of Georgia.

1998   John gets his pilot's license in April, a feat he had dreamed about since childhood.

1999   John, his wife, Carolyn, and his sister-in-law, Lauren Bessette, die on July 16 when the plane John is piloting crashes into the Atlantic off Cape Cod.

Source Notes

Chapter 1
1. Angie Cannon and Peter Cory, "The Final Hours," *U.S. News & World Report*, August 2, 1999, p. 20.
2. Sharon Begley, "A Spiral into the Sea," *Newsweek*, Memorial Issue, Summer/Fall, 1999, p. 58.
3. Angie Cannon and Peter Cory, p. 19.
4. Ibid., p. 20.
5. Ibid., p. 18.
6. Erica Noonan, "JFK Jr. Plane Debris Found," *The Atlanta Journal-Constitution*, July 18, 1999, p. A1.
7. Tyler Mallory, "Lost in the Night," *People Weekly*, August 2, 1999, p. 54.
8. Quoted in Erica Noonan.
9. S.D. Reed, Kyle Smith, and Jill Smolove, *John F. Kennedy Jr.: A Biography*. New York: Time Inc., 1999, p. 119.
10. Angie Cannon and Peter Cory, p. 22.
11. Ibid.
12. Tyler Mallory, "Lost in the Night," p. 56.
13. Sharon Begley, "A Desperate Search," *Newsweek*, July 26, 1999, p. 36.
14. Nancy Gibbs, "…The Lost Horizon," *Time*, July 26, 1999, p. 29.

15. "Searchers Find Clues But No Answers in Search for JFK Jr.'s Plane," *CNN Larry King Weekend*, July 18, 1999. Transcript.
16. Sharon Begley, "A Desperate Search," p. 34.
17. Tyler Mallory, "Lost in the Night," p. 57.
18. "Senator Recalls Nephew Who Treasured Legacy," *The New York Times*, July 24, 1999, p. A12.

Chapter 2
1. Wendy Leigh, *Prince Charming: The John F. Kennedy Jr. Story.* New York: Signet, 1999, p. 21.
2. Peter Collier and David Horowitz, *The Kennedys: An American Dream.* New York: Summit Books, 1984, p. 150.
3. Jacques Lowe, *Jacqueline Kennedy Onassis: The Making of a First Lady.* Santa Monica, CA: General Publishing Group, 1996, p. 18.
4. Wendy Leigh, p. 38.
5. "JFK Jr. Plane Missing," *CNN Live Event Special,* July 17, 1999. Transcript.
6. Wendy Leigh, p. 46.
7. J.D. Reed, Kyle Smith, and Jill Smolove, *John F. Kennedy Jr.: A Biography*, p. 23.
8. "Senator Recalls Nephew Who Treasured Legacy."
9. Wendy Leigh, p. 53.
10. Barbara Kantrowitz, "The Last Child of Camelot," *Newsweek*, August 2, 1999, p. 36.
11. Carl Sferrazza Anthony. *As We Remember Her: Jacqueline Kennedy Onassis in the Words of Her Friends and Family.* New York: HarperCollins, 1997, p. 157.
12. Edward Klein, *All Too Human: The Love Story of Jack and Jackie Kennedy.* New York: Pocket Books, 1996, p. 287.
13. Carl Sferrazza Anthony, p. 157.
14. Jerry Adler, "There's Just the Three of Us," *Newsweek*, Memorial Edition, Summer/Fall, 1999, p. 30.
15. Carl Sferrazza Anthony, p. 158.
16. Jerry Adler, p. 31.
17. Wendy Leigh, p. 60.
18. Ibid., p. 39.
19. Ibid., p. 47.
20. Ibid., p. 40.
21. "The White House Years," *People Weekly*, Commemorative Issue, Summer 1999, p. 5.

22. Edward Klein, p. 339.
23. Ibid.
24. J.D. Reed, Kyle Smith, and Jill Smolove, p. 13.
25. Wendy Leigh, p. 59
26. Jerry Adler, p. 33.
27. Wendy Leigh, p. 17.
28. John H. Davis, *The Kennedys: Dynasty and Disaster.* New York: Shapolsky Publishers, 1992, p. 160.
29. Peter Collier and David Horowitz, p. 193.
30. Jerry Adler, p. 36.
31. Ibid.
32. Wendy Leigh, p. 65.
33. Richard Reeves, *President Kennedy: Profile of Power.* New York: Simon & Schuster, 1993, p. 553.
34. Ibid., p. 662.
35. "The White House Years," *People Weekly*, Commemorative Issue.

Chapter 3
1. Christopher Andersen, *Jackie After Jack: Portrait of a Lady.* New York: William Morrow, 1998, p. 59.
2. J.D. Reed, Kyle Smith, and Jill Smolove, *John F. Kennedy Jr.: A Biography*, p. 27.
3. Ibid., p. 30.
4. Christopher Anderson, p. 96.
5. "In Public, In Private: A Photo Album," *Newsweek*, Memorial Edition, Summer/Fall, 1999, p. 21.
6. "Good Morning America," *ABC News*, July 23, 1999. Transcript #3519.
7. Wendy Leigh, *Prince Charming*, p. 117.
8. Jerry Adler, p. 36.
9. Ibid.
10. Tyler Mallory "Guiding Light," *People Weekly*, August 2, 1999, p. 79.
11. Christopher Andersen, p. 155.
12. J.D. Reed, Kyle Smith, and Jill Smolove, p. 33.
13. Jerry Adler, p. 39.
14. J.D. Reed, Kyle Smith, and Jill Smolove, p. 38.
15. Ibid.
16. Ibid., p. 39.
17. Rose Fitzgerald Kennedy, *Times to Remember*, New York: Doubleday, 1995, p. 412.

18. Christopher Andersen, p. 195.
19. J.D. Reed, Kyle Smith, and Jill Smolove, p. 38.
20. Christopher Andersen, p. 201.
21. Ibid., p. 217.
22. Tyler Mallory, "Guiding Light," p. 80.
23. Ibid., p. 81.
24. J.D. Reed, Kyle Smith, and Jill Smolove, p. 41.
25. Ibid.
26. Wendy Leigh, p. 158.
27. Ibid.
28. Ibid., p. 150.
29. Eric Pooley, "The Art of Being JFK Jr.," *Time*, July 26, 1999, p. 38.
30. Wendy Leigh, p. 169.
31. Ibid.
32. "Good Morning America."
33. Ibid.

Chapter 4
1. "Good Morning America," *ABC News*.
2. Tyler Mallory, "Guiding Light," p. 81.
3. Wendy Leigh, *Prince Charming*, p. 183.
4. Ibid., p. 187.
5. "JFK Jr. 1960–1999: Friends Reflect on Lives Cut Tragically Short," *CNN Larry King Live*, July 19, 1999. Transcript.
6. Wendy Leigh, p. 190.
7. Ibid.
8. Ibid., p. 191.
9. Ibid., p. 204.
10. Ibid., p. 194.
11. "JFK Jr. 1960–1999: Friends Reflect on Lives Cut Tragically Short." *CNN Larry King Live*, July 19, 1999. Transcript.
12. J.D. Reed, Kyle Smith, and Jill Smolove, *John F. Kennedy Jr.: A Biography*, p. 48.
13. Ibid. p. 49.
14. Tyler Mallory, "Guiding Light," p. 80.
15. Ibid.
16. Ibid.
17. "JFK Jr. Plane Missing: Friends Discuss Their Relationship With JFK Jr.," *CNN Larry King Weekend*, July 17, 1999. Transcript.
18. J.D. Reed, Kyle Smith, and Jill Smolove, p. 50.

19. Wendy Leigh, p. 227.
20. J.D. Reed, Kyle Smith, and Jill Smolove, p. 50.
21. Wendy Leigh, p. 227.
22. Christopher Andersen, *Jackie After Jack: Portrait of a Lady,* p. 351.
23. Ibid.
24. J.D. Reed, Kyle Smith, and Jill Smolove, p. 50.
25. Wendy Leigh, p. 241.

Chapter 5
1. J.D. Reed, Kyle Smith, and Jill Smolove, *John F. Kennedy Jr.: A Biography*, p. 75.
2. Ibid.
3. "Boy to Man," *People Weekly*, Commemorative Issue, Summer, 1999, p. 41.
4. Tyler Mallory, "Two of a Kind," *People Weekly*, August 2, 1999, p. 85.
5. Jerry Adler, p. 28.
6. J.D. Reed, Kyle Smith, and Jill Smolove, p. 76.
7. Ibid., p. 56.
8. Ibid., p. 57.
9. Wendy Leigh, p. 284.
10. "JFK Jr. Plane Missing," *CNN Live Event Special,* July 17, 1999. Transcript.
11. J.D. Reed, Kyle Smith, and Jill Smolove, p. 93.
12. "JFK Jr. Plane Missing," *CNN Larry King Weekend*, July 18, 1999. Transcript.

Chapter 6
1. Weston Kosova, "A Celebrity Goes to Work," *Newsweek*, Memorial Edition, Summer/Fall, 1999, p. 50.
2. John F. Kennedy Jr. "Editor's Letter — 10/95," *George*, October 1999, p. 148.
3. "JFK Jr. Plane Missing: Friends Discuss Their Relationship With JFK Jr." *CNN Larry King Weekend*, July 17, 1999. Transcript.
4. J.D. Reed, Kyle Smith, and Jill Smolove, *John F. Kennedy Jr.: A Biography*, p. 107.
5. Ibid.
6. Ibid., p. 108.

7. Lynette Clementson and Dorinda Elliot, "The Woman Who Won His Heart," *Newsweek*, July 26, 1999, p. 44.
8. John Leland, "They Had Instant Eye Contact," *Newsweek*, Memorial Edition, Summer/Fall, 1999, p. 42.
9. Ibid.
10. "Soulmates," *People Weekly*, Commemorative Issue, Summer 1999, p. 61.
11. J.D. Reed, Kyle Smith, and Jill Smolove, p. 115.
12. Lynette Clementson and Dorinda Elliot, p. 45.
13. Tyler Mallory, "A Man in Full," *People Weekly*, August 2, 1999, p. 67.

Chapter 7
1. "JFK Jr. Plane Missing: Friends Discuss Their Relationship With JFK Jr." *CNN Larry King Weekend*, July 17, 1999. Transcript.
2. Jerry Adler, p. 30.
3. Evan Thomas, "Living With the Myth," *Newsweek*, July 26, 1999, p. 42.
4. Ibid.
5. "Senator Recalls Nephew Who Treasured Legacy." *The New York Times*, July 24, 1999, p. A12.

Further Reading

Andersen, Catherine Corley, *Jackie Kennedy Onassis: Woman of Courage*. Minneapolis: Lerner, 1995.

Blue, Rose and Naden, Corinne J. *The White House Kids*. Brookfield, CT: The Millbrook Press, 1996.

Goodwin, Doris Kearns. *The Fitzgeralds and the Kennedys*. New York: St. Martin's Press, 1991.

Mills, Judie. *Robert F. Kennedy*. Brookfield, CT: The Millbrook Press, 1998.

Mills, Judie. *John F. Kennedy*. New York: Franklin Watts, 1988.

Pietrusua, David. *John F. Kennedy*. San Diego, CA: Lucent Books, 1997.

Sandak, Cass R. *The Kennedys*. New York: Crestwood House, 1991.

Schulman, Arlene. *Robert F. Kennedy: Promise for the Future*. New York: Facts On File, 1998.

Simonelli, Susan Beale. *Rose Kennedy*. New York: Chelsea House, 1992.

Trask, Richard B. *That Day in Dallas: Three Photographers Capture on Film the Day President Kennedy Died*. Danvers, MA: Yeoman Press, 1998.

Uschan, Michael V. *The Importance of John F. Kennedy*. San Diego, CA: Lucent Books, 1999.

Index